U.S. MARINE CORPS
AVIATION UNIT INSIGNIA
1941-1946

THE AUTHOR

Jeff Millstein was born in New York City. He joined the Marine Corps in 1957 and served until 1964. After receiving his bachelors in 1963 and masters in marketing in 1967, Jeff went to work as an advertising manager for Peterson Publishing Company. He then became account management supervisor at Doyle Dan Burnbach Advertising.

Mr. Millstein founded Briarcliff Classic & Imported Car Service in 1970 having raced sports cars, SCCA, since 1963. He continued racing until 1979 when he sold his car business. Jeff Millstein & Associates, a marketing company, was founded in 1979. Then in 1990, Jeff started another company called Air Cleaning Equipment Company.

He lives in Westtown, NY with his wife, Allison, and their two children, Kate and Anna. He pursues interests in WWII military aviation history, collecting aviation patches, writing, architecture, collecting antiques, old toys, toy soldiers, toy trains, old toy sailboats and Eskimo stone carvings.

Mr. Millstein has previously had articles published in Leatherneck Magazine, Sports Car Graphic Magazine, Air Force Museum Magazine and Old Toy Soldier Magazine. He is proud to present his *U.S. Marine Corps Aviation Unit Insignia 1941-1946* collector's book to all Marines and collectors.

TURNER PUBLISHING COMPANY

This book or any part thereof may not be
reproduced by any means, mechanical or electronic,
without written consent of Turner Publishing Company

Library of Congress Catalog Card No.
95-60546
ISBN: 978-1-68162-376-4

Editor: Amy Cloud
Designer: Luke Henry

Copyright © 1995
Turner Publishing Company

Additional books available from
Turner Publishing Company, Paducah, Kentucky

Contents

Introduction

This book, *U.S. Marine Corps Aviation Insignia 1941-1946*, is the result of a great deal of effort and excellent work by Jeff Millstein and is sure to create a great many intensive discussions (arguments) among members of Marine Aviation Units of World War II. During this period, the insignia was often changed, i.e. unit numbers, aircraft and designations, VMF or VMA. All experienced changes in personnel, groups, wings, etc.

When one is transferred from one unit to another, from staff to flying or flying to staff, it all became very confusing and many did not retain the original patch or worry about it at that time. It is interesting to visit a museum where many patches are displayed and to listen to the discussions that result from the display and to hear the high percentage of former squadron members (or family members) who now "want to get a copy of their insignia." The display at the Fighter Aces Museum at Mesa, Arizona was where I first found my squadron patch after the War.

This book will serve to bring back great memories for actual participants and also provide a great memento for the families of these members. My congratulations to Jeff for doing an "Outstanding Job."

B/Gen. Robert E. Galer, USMC (ret.)

Preface

I guess you could say that I began writing this book back in the spring of 1942, shortly after my father enlisted in the Army Air Corps as a flight surgeon. As a little boy, I travelled from base to base as the family followed my father from one duty assignment to another. The memories of this time are still vivid. The best of times.

I had an olive drab snowsuit complete with master sergeant's stripes and "hashmarks" on it for weekday wear, the same one I wore when my dad took me up for my first airplane ride in a B–17 Flying Fortress bomber. My dad flew every month for the extra flight pay he needed in order for his family to survive as housing around military bases didn't come cheap. Some officers thought it chic to bring their dogs along. My father brought me. Usually I flew the nose gunner's position. My mother had

The author with his trusty (1000 shot Thompson sub-machine) gun ,which never had to be reloaded, pistol belt and wearing standard issue "V" (V for victory) t-shirt.

me grounded when she found out about my flight status. She had this thing about her four year old belonging in bombers. What did she know???

I also had a set of officer's "pinks & greens" to wear for Sunday dinners at the O Club. As the "Major's kid" you enjoy certain privileges. All sorts of nice sergeants kept giving me stuff...insignia, souvenirs, a hand carved Tommy Gun. I learned to love Spam and Vienna Sausages and C–Ration beef stew.

All the men in our family served in the war. Cousin Stan was a radioman gunner on B–25 straffer aircraft with the 345th Bomb (Air Apaches) Group in the South Pacific. Cousin Sy served on Nimitz's and Halsey's staff as an interpreter because he spoke fluent Japanese from his days in the import–export business prior to the war. His brother, Saul, flew as a pilot with VMSB–144 during the Guadalcanal Campaign. All of them contributed to my "hoard of artifacts" as they returned from combat duties.

We were stationed at Miami Beach in late 1943, when the War Department took over the hotels to use as hospitals and "flak houses" for returning casualties from the air war in North Africa and England. My dad was the medical officer in charge of the Cadillac Hotel. I remember my Cousin Saul showing up one day in his dress whites, fresh from the "Canal", 40–50 lbs thinner, his skin a nice atabrine yellow from the anti–malarial drugs they took out in the islands. He gave me a Japanese sword and a pistol. My mother wouldn't let me keep the hand grenade he had with him. A friend of my father's, from his medical school days at Yale, came back from the China–Burma–India theater. Another load of goodies.

I remember the War Department setting up a war bond museum. They just blocked off a couple of streets, filled it with captured Japanese Zeros and German Stukas, and sold war bonds to the people who toured the display. I got some more good stuff from the friendly sergeants who ran it, a German stick grenade, an Italian helmet, and a Japanese meatball flag.

When the war ended these artifacts continued on as part of everyday play. All the kids in the neighborhood had dads who had served in WW2 and we reenacted the war with authentic gear. We dug trenches and foxholes in a local New York City park. We trapped a Parks Department truck in one of our camoflaged tank traps. We tossed cherry bomb firecrackers into subway entrances which became the Japanese caves we saw in "Guadalcanal Diary". Our favorite line was the one snarled by Anthony Quinn as he hurled a knife into the back of a Japanese soldier who was running away...."Hey Jap, you forgot something!". We dropped rocks off the George Washington Bridge at the boats passing below in the Hudson River to simulate bombing attacks against shipping. My school books filled with pencil drawings of P–40s shooting down

Zeros. We wore war surplus clothing. We used war surplus web gear in the Boy Scouts. During hikes, our troop looked like Merrill's Marauders, just before they were declared unfit for further combat.

Then I grew up and joined the Marine Corps. My mother, like all mothers, "cleaned" my room out while I was at Parris Island. I'm convinced she was waiting and dreaming of this opportunity for at least ten years. When I returned home on boot leave my room looked as though I'd never lived there. It was empty. It smelled from hospital disinfectant. I asked her why she threw everything out she said that "Men don't play with

The author as an 18 year old Marine.

those things." But she missed one box. It was tucked away in a spot she'd forgotten to look. It was the box that contained my patches. She hadn't severed my connection to WW2.

Years later, while working at an ad agency, I began to really appreciate the designs of the squadron insignia. Some were obviously Marine but I had no way to identify them. No one really knew anymore and there would be a time that it would be impossible to ever find out. I asked long time patch collectors. I bothered the hell out of John Elliott, a retired Marine major who served with VMSB 341 and author of a series of books on U.S. Navy – Marine Corps Aircraft Markings, as well as the rest of the staff at the office of Naval Aviation History and Archives who helped as much as they could. Mrs. Rich never dodged my calls.

It became obvious that there was no definitive record and probably never would be unless one was developed. After all, Pearl Harbor Day, December 7th, a day long held sacred in my family, wasn't even being remembered on the 6 O'Clock News any more. When I complained to a good friend, Manny Scoulas, that this information was pretty close to being lost forever, he encouraged me to produce a record while the people who created the history were still around to talk to.

I approached the Marine Corps Historical Foundation with a concept that a research project be initiated to locate, identify, and produce a four color record of these logos. They gave me a research grant to do so and I began a nine year project to locate personnel in each of the squadrons to develop the information. During the interviews, I amassed a record of background data as to the meanings of the symbols, names of artists, etc. As word of the project spread, collectors like Bob Gill, George Menagaux, Bob Byrd, Bob Queen, Tom Fitzgerald, Doug Bailey (all former Marines themselves) Dave Hill, and John Bozich were quick to help. Bill Scott, a military collectibles dealer would call every time he got a patch that he thought belonged to a Marine Aviation unit. And my fellow marines, who were not collectors, helped out. Every request for information in Leatherneck Magazine always generated a lot of responses. If the writers didn't know, they sent the names of others who might. Along the way I got the chance to make friends with Hank Sory, Mule Holmberg, Doc Everton, and Rex Hamilton; the kind you'd call up just to shoot the breeze and exchange Christmas cards with -friends who understood the importance of the project and provided a lot of help. Sadly Doc and Rex aren't here to see the finished book. I never realized that their time was so short. I never questioned that they wouldn't be here forever.

As the project went along I became more and more convinced that the visual and written data should be combined in published form for easy public access, rather than allowing it to disappear into the archives, to be remembered only by scholars. And that's how this book got to be written.

Lest we forget.

Prologue

During WWI Marine Corps Aviation personnel used a shoulder sleeve insignia. Marine Corps aviation unit insignia first came into use during the mid 1920's with the Ace Of Spades insignia of the 1st Air Squadron and the Running Red Devil insignia of VF-3M.

Shoulder sleeve insignia worn by aviation personnel in WWII.

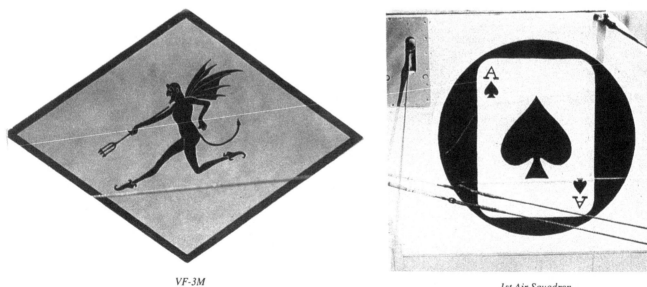

VF-3M   *1st Air Squadron*

Marine aviation continued on into the 30's as a very small contingent within a very small branch of service, so small that only an additional five designs were created by 1939.

VJ-7M — VMJ-2.

VO-9M.

VJ-7M, Aircraft 2, MAG-21.

Major Wallace wearing Aircraft One insignia above the name strip on his jacket, standing in front of a BG-1.

Aircraft One.

NAS Long Beach, 1940. Bruce Porter wearing Long Beach Air Station insignia on his flight jacket, next to an aircraft with the same insignia on the fuselage.

NAS San Diego, 1926. Curtiss pursuit with Running Red Devil insignia on the fuselage just forward of the tail section.

NAS San Diego, 1926. Formation flying. Ace of Spades insignia now located on fuselage forward of tail section.

1928, Douglas OD-1 assigned to VJ-7M.

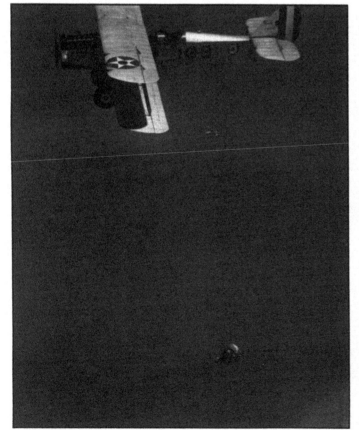

NAS San Diego, 1926. Parachute jump from Ace of Spades squadron aircraft, parachute just opening.

Brown Field, January 1927. Curtiss F6C-3 assigned to VF-1M with J.E. Brown ready for takeoff on a cold winter day.

NAS San Diego, 1926. VO-1 D.H. (De Havaland) lined up for inspection. Note squadron insignia on vertical stabilizer.

And then came December 7th, 1941, the sneak Japanese attack on Pearl Harbor. Marine Corps response to the attack was an almost immediate expansion of the Air Wing. Fourteen VMF, nine VMSB, and two VMD squadrons were commissioned in 1942 alone. And these figures don't come close to reflecting the number of aviation support units that were formed to sustain combat operations and train replacement flight personnel. By war's end over 125,000 personnel had served in Marine Aviation.

Unit: MAG-23
Date Commissioned: 3.1.42
Date Decommissioned: 11.1.45
Nickname of Unit: n/a
Name of Artist: Walt Disney Studios
Date of Insignia: 1942
Authorization: HQMC
Remarks: none
Acknowledgements: none
Manufacturing Details: Decal on leather.

Marine Air Group-23

Unit: MAG-25
Date Commissioned: 6.1.42
Date Decommissioned: 5.31.47
Nickname of Unit: SCAT
Name of Artist: Walt Disney Studio
Date of Insignia: 1942
Authorization: HQMC
Type of Aircraft Employed: R4D
Remarks: The motto, Securite En Nuages, literally translated means safety in the clouds, the only place to be when flying a R4D chased by a Zero.
Acknowledgements: Robert J. Biggane
Manufacturing Details: Australian embroidered on wool.

Marine Air Group -25

Unit: MAG-41
Date Commissioned: 9.15.43 as MBDAG 41 (Marine Base Defense Group 41), changed to MAG 41 11.10.43.
Date Decommissioned: 10.31.45
Nickname of Unit: n/a
Name of Artist: Walt Disney Studios
Date of Insignia: December 1943
Authorization: HQMC
Type of Aircraft Employed: n/a
Acknowledgements: Mule Holmberg
Manufacturing Details: painted on aileron fabric.

Marine Air Defense Group - 41.

Unit: MAG-51
Date Commissioned: 1.1.44
Date Decommissioned: 2.20.46
Nickname of Unit: none
Name of Artist: n/a
Date of Insignia: n/a
Authorization: HQMC
Remarks: none
Acknowledgements: Maj. John Elliott, USMC (RET.)
Manufacturing Details: PX patch.

Marine Air Group-51.

Unit: VMJ-2
Date Commissioned: 5.2.45
Date Deactivated: 3.6.46
Nickname of Unit: n/a
Name of Artist: n/a
Date of Insignia: 1945
Authorization: local
Type of Aircraft Employed: JM-1
Remarks: The insignia is a spread of six cards, ace thru nine, in spades. Each aircraft had this painted on the nose just forward of the pilot"s compartment. One card was assigned to each of the six squadron aircraft. A large spade was painted on the tail with the assigned card designation.
Acknowledgements: Jack Hilburn, William Drewitz, K.K. Biglow

MAG-51 unidentified crew members wearing group insignia on flight jackets.

Martin JM-1 with VMJ-2 nose insignia and individual aircraft insignia on tail.

Unit: VMS-3
Date Commissioned: 1934 as VMO-9, redesignated
    VMS-3 1.7.37
Date Deactivated: 5.20.44
Nickname of Unit: n/a
Name of Artist: Capt. Hayne D. Boyden
Date of Insignia: n/a
Authorization: HQMC
Type of Aircraft Employed: n/a
Remarks: none
Acknowledgements: none

VMS-3.

Unit: VMJ-3
Date Commissioned: 5.1.45
Date Deactivated: 10.21.45
Nickname of Unit: Black Jacks or Red Asses
Name of Artist: S/Sgt. Charles Lawrenson
Date of Insignia: 1945
Authorization: HQMC
Type of Aircraft Employed: JM-1
Remarks: The donkey in the insignia was chosen be-
    cause of it's fame as a "beast of burden" in pull-
    ing things. Originally it had red hindquarters be-
    cause many of the aircraft had their tails shot up
    during target towing. The donkey with the red
    hindquarters appeared on squadron signs and air-
    craft. The red hindquarters were deleted from the
    official insignia at the direction of HQMC and
    did not appear in the jacket patch.
Acknowledgements: L/Col. Thomas Wood USMC
    (ret.), Former Sargent Glen Duncan, Richard M.
    Pettigrew.
Manufacturing Details: American embroidered on
    wool.

Cpl. Walter G. Scott standing in front of squadron sign with "red posterior."

VMJ-3.

Shot up tail on squadron aircraft showing reason for the donkey's red posterior.

Reverse view of same aircraft showing damage.

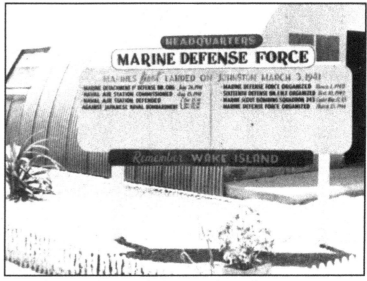

"Remember Wake Island" sign on Johnston Island.

VMJ-3 aircraft in formation, two without completed tail markings, one with.

JM-1 "The Red Ass" with squadron insignia painted on nose.

VMJ-3 Squadron aircraft with incomplete markings.

VMJ-3 Squadron aircraft with tail markings only.

Unit: VMO-1
Date Commissioned: 10.27.43
Date Deactivated: 1.12.44
Nickname of Unit: n/a
Name of Artist: S/Sgt. F.F. Lobeck
Date of Insignia: 1943
Authorization: HQMC
Type of Aircraft Employed: OY-1
Remarks: The significance of the design was derived from the nickname for the artillery spotting aircraft which were called "Grasshoppers" due to their ability to fly in and out of improvised fields. The field glasses and artillery shell denote their primary mission of artillery spotting.
Acknowledgements: none
Manufacturing Details: Fully embroidered, possibly Japanese during occupation.

VMO-1.

Unit: VMO-2
Date Commissioned: 1.12.44
Date Deactivated: 8.26.46
Nickname of Unit: n/a
Name of Artist: S/Sgt. F.F. Lobeck
Date of Insignia: 1944
Authorization: HQMC
Type of Aircraft Employed: OY-1
Remarks: The significance of the design was derived from the nickname for the artillery spotting airplanes which were called "Grasshoppers" due to their ability to get in and out of small improvised fields. The field glasses denoted their primary mission as an artillery spotter.
Acknowledgements: John Frech.

VMO-2.

VMO-3.

Unit: VMO-3
Date Commissioned: 1.12.44
Date Deactivated: n/a
Nickname of Unit: n/a
Name of Artist: S/Sgt. F.F. Lobeck
Date of Insignia: February 1944
Authorization: HQMC
Type of Aircraft Employed: OY-1
Remarks: The significance of the design was derived from the nickname for the artillery spotting airplanes which were called "Grasshoppers" due to their ability to fly or literally hop out of small improvised fields. The field glasses and cannon denote their primary mission as artillery spotters.
Acknowledgements: Jerry Zajic, Stanislaus Antos, Jerry Brinkman
Manufacturing Details: Silk-screened on canvas with embroidered edge. PX patch.

VMO-4

Unit: VMO-4
Date Commissioned: 1.12.44
Date Deactivated: 10.21.45
Nickname of Unit: n/a
Name of Artist: S/Sgt. F.F. Lobeck
Date of Insignia: 1944
Authorization: HQMC
Type of Aircraft Employed: OY-1
Remarks: The significance of the design was derived from the nickname for the artillery spotting airplanes which were called "Grasshoppers" due to their ability to fly in and out of improvised fields. The field glasses and artillery shell denote their primary mission of artillery spotting.
Acknowledgements: L/Col. Don Blaha USMC(ret.)
Manufacturing Details: Embroidered on cotton cloth.

VMO-5

Unit: VMO-5
Date Commissioned: 2.15.44
Date Deactivated: 1.31.46
Nickname of Unit: n/a
Name of Artist: S/Sgt. F.F. Lobeck
Date of Insignia: February 1944
Authorization: HQMC
Type of Aircraft Employed: OY-1
Remarks: The significance of the design was derived from the nickname of the artillery spotting airplanes which were called "Grasshoppers" due to their ability to fly from improvised fields. The field glasses note their primary mission of aerial observation for artillery fire. The skull denotes their effect upon the enemy.
Acknowledgements: none

Unit: VMO-6
Date Commissioned: 11.20.44
Date Deactivated: n/a
Nickname of Unit: n/a
Name of Artist: S/Sgt. F.F. Lobeck
Date of Insignia: 1944
Authorization: HQMC
Type of Aircraft Employed: OY-1
Remarks: The significance of the design was derived from the nickname of the artillery spotting airplanes which were called "Grasshoppers" due to their ability to fly from improvised fields. The field glasses denote their primary mission of aerial observation of artillery fire. The lit firecracker was the explosion that would occur.
Acknowledgements: none
Manufacturing Details: American embroidered on wool.

VMO-6.

The "Last Chance" pilot quarters on Roi.

Standing L-R: Lt. G. "George" Manitz, Lt. R.E. "Smokey" Stitt, Lt. H.T. "Tony" Burns, kneeling L-R: Lt. J.W. "Woody" Wood, Lt. W.H. "Doc" Magill, Lt. L.L. "Slick" Irwin.

VMF-111.

Unit: VMF-111
Date Commissioned: 7.7.41
Date Deactivated: 11.26.45
Nickname of Unit: n/a
Name of Artist: n/a
Date of Insignia: n/a
Authorization: HQMC
Type of Aircraft Employed: F4F-3, SNJ-3, J2F-5, F4F-4, SNJ-4, F4U-1, F4U-1D, SBD-6
Remarks: none
Acknowledgements: none
Manufacturing Details: Hand painted on fabric.

VMF-111.

VMF-111 pilots, taken on Roi.

Proposed insignia produced for VMF-112 personnel who eventually became nucleus of VMF-214 under the command of Maj. Boyington. From the Marine Corps Historical Foundation Collection.

VMF-112 First Design.

Unit: VMF-112
Date Commissioned: 3.1.42
Date Deactivated: 9.10.45
Nickname of Unit: Wolfpack
Name of Artist: Lt. Hugo A. Olsson
Date of Insignia: 1942
Authorization: HQMC
Type of Aircraft Employed: F2A-2, F4F-3, F4F-4, F4U-1, FG-1
Remarks: During the first combat tour on Guadalcanal in November 1942 Lt. Hugo Olsson developed several designs for a proposed squadron insignia. The executive officer, Maj. Paul Fontana, named the squadron the "Wolfpack" after his alma mater, the University of Nevada. The University of Nevada's athletic emblem is a wolf's head and Lt. Olsson incorporated it into what became the squadron's official insignia. Patches with "VMF 112" in an arc at the top and "Wolfpack" in an arc at the bottom were made for flight personnel during an R&R in Australia. Both blue and white backgrounds were used. The squadron returned to the United States in September 1943 for reorganization and training as a carrier squadron. During this period the original design was modified to exclude all references to unit identity. Patches were issued to all personnel for wear. The background was white only.
Acknowledgements: Norman Ebell, Col. J.B. Maas USMC(ret.), John O'Neill, Hugo Olsson, B/Gen. Paul Fontana USMC(ret.), James Sykes.
Manufacturing Details: First issue - Australian embroidered on wool. Second issue - American embroidered on wool.

VMF-112 First Design.

VMF-112 Second Design.

VMF-112 squadron photo with "Wolf Pack" sign board.

VMF-113.

Unit: VMF-113
Date Commissioned: 1.1.43
Date Deactivated: 4.30.47
Nickname of Unit: Whistling Devils
Name of Artist: Walt Disney Studios
Date of Insignia: 1943
Authorization: HQMC
Type of Aircraft Employed: F4F-3, F4U-1, FM-1,
    SNJ-4, FG-1D, F4U-1D
Remarks: none
Acknowledgements: Philip White, Col. Loren Everton
    USMC (ret), Rex Hamilton, Shelby Forrest
Manufacturing Details: American embroidered on
    wool.

VMF-113 Maj. L.D. "Doc" Everton standing left of VMF-113 sign, standing right of sign L-R Capt. E.O. Anglin, Capt. Frank C. Drury, Lt. Joe V. Shellack, Kneeling, right of sign L-R MTSgt Pete Tunno, MTS Sgt Bernard Nelson.

Unit: VMF-114
Date Commissioned: 9.15.43
Date Deactivated: transitioned to VMF(N)114 8.1.47
Nickname of Unit: Death Dealers
Name of Artist: Capt. Robert F. Stout, Squadron CO
Date of Insignia: 1943
Authorization: Local
Type of Aircraft Employed: F4U-1
Remarks: The playing cards depicted in the insignia served two functions. When placed next to "VMF" the Ace-Ace-Four configuration serves as the Unit's numerical designation. The "Aces Over Eights" were also the cards dealt to Wild Bill Hickock the night he was shot by Jack McCall and known as the "Dead Man's Hand". As the insignia was designed by Capt. Robert "Cowboy" Stout whose home address was Wyoming, the choice of symbols was probably related to his background. The insignia was produced for wear in very limited numbers and issued to flight personnel only. Later, when the squadron ceased operations and returned to the United States, the insignia was issued to all hands, this time without "Death Dealers" in the banner at the bottom.
Acknowledgements: Robert Tucker, Harry Murphy
Manufacturing Details: First issue - Australian embroidered on wool. Second issue - silk screen on canvas.

VMF-114 first design.

VMF-114 second design.

VMF-114 Peleliu, 1944. Left Unknown, TSgt Harry Murphy on right.

VMF-115. Patch made in China, 1946.

VMF-115, second design.

VMF-115 Maj. Joe Foss wearing G-1 flight jacket with first issue painted insignia.

Unit: VMF-115

Date Commissioned: 9.15.43, changed to VMF(AW) 12.31.56, to VMFA 1.1.64

Date Deactivated: still active

Nickname of Unit: Joe's Jokers

Name of Artist: Walt Disney Studios

Date of Insignia: August 1943

Authorization: HQMC

Type of Aircraft Employed: F4U-1, F4U-1D, FG-1, FG-1D

Remarks: The insignia originally designed by the Disney Studios for VMF-115 featured a comic rendering of an F4U smoking a cigar which referred to the aircraft flown by the squadron and the ever present "stogie" of its skipper Joe Foss. Eventually, when the nickname Joe's Jokers caught on, the original design became the Joker card in a hand of five cards.

Acknowledgements: Col. Robert t. Kingsbury USMC (Ret.), Col. John King USMC(Ret.)

Manufacturing Details: First issue - painted on leather. Paint flaked badly from the leather patch. Patches were removed from jackets and exchanged for cloth version. Second issue - Australian embroidered on wool. Third issue - Chinese made on silk.

Unit: VMF-121
Date Commissioned: 7.7.41
Date Deactivated: 9.9.45,
Reactivated: 3.1.51, changed to VMA 5.15.51,
    still active.
Nickname of Unit: n/a
Name of Artist: Lt. Hugo Olsson
Date of Insignia: August 1942
Authorization: HQMC
Type of Aircraft Employed: F4F-4, SNJ-3, F4U-1,
    FG-1, F4U-1D, FG-1D
Remarks: The first insignia was stencilled on flight
    gear. Patches were made for the flight personnel
    during an R&R in Australia. When the squadron
    returned to the United States for re-organization
    and retraining, patches were made for all hands.
    These insignia were the same in all respects ex-
    cept that the "VMF-121" was deleted from the
    design.
Acknowledgements: Hugo A Olsson, Col. Robert
    Bryson USMC(Ret.)
Manufacturing Details: First issue - Australian em-
    broidered on wool. Second issue - American em-
    broidered on wool.

VMF-121.

Unit: VMF-122
Date Commissioned: 2.28.42, changed to VMF(AW)
    10.10.62, to VMFA 7.1.65
Date Deactivated: still active
Nickname of Unit: n/a
Name of Artist: Kayo Tojo insignia-unknown Austra-
    lian Wolf On Whiskey Bottle-Sgt. Jack L. Rafalsky
Date of Insignia: Kayo Tojo-1942 Wolf On whiskey
    Bottle-1943
Authorization: Kayo Tojo-local Wolf On Whiskey
    Bottle-HQMC
Type of Aircraft Employed: F4F-4, SNJ-3, F3A-1,
    F4U-1, FG-1, F4U-1D, FG-1D
Remarks: VMF-122's first insignia was developed and
    manufactured during an R&R to Sydney Austra-
    lia. Produced in a very limited number, distribu-
    tion was limited to flight personnel only. The "of-
    ficial" insignia was designed and manufactured
    when the squadron returned to the United States
    for re-organization and retraining. The "Wolf
    Riding A Whiskey Bottle" design was manufac-
    tured as insignia with "VMF-122" below the whis-
    key bottle. Both ends of the whiskey bottle ex-
    tended past the edges of the disk. Another run of
    insignia was produced where all references to
    VMF-122 were deleted and the artwork was re-
    duced in size and centered on a brown background.
Acknowledgements: Philip White, Col. John P.
    McMahon USMC(Ret.), W.R. Cousins, Col.
    Herbert "Trigger" Long USMC(Ret.), Former 1st.
    Sgt.Thomas Abourezk, Jack Mohedano.
Manufacturing Details: Kayo Tojo - Australian em-
    broidered on wool. First issue Wolf On Whiskey
    bottle - American embroidered on wool. Second
    issue Wolf On Whiskey Bottle - decal on leather.

VMF-122 First Design.

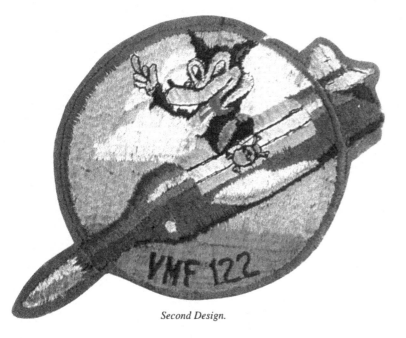

Second Design.

Third Design.

VMF-123.

Unit: VMF-123
Date Commissioned: 9.7.42
Date Deactivated: 9.10.45
Nickname of Unit: Eight Balls
Name of Artist: Col. Robert Steinkraus USMC(Ret.)
Date of Insignia: 1943
Authorization: HQMC
Type of Aircraft Employed: F4F-3P, F4F-4, J2F-5, SNJ-3, F3A-1, FG-1
Remarks: In Naval Aviation Training Dilbert was an accident looking for a place to happen. VMF-123 had made two tours to combat without seeing any enemy aircraft. Morale was low and the squadron was beginning to feel that they were a bunch of eightballs. A couple of pilots with some artistic talent drew an eightball with Dilbert looking over the top from the rear and this began to appear on signs. The third tour was a lot different from the first two with Zeros and Vals in abundance. Upon their return to Efate and before going on R&R the emblem was redrawn with Dilbert in front of the eightball. The original patches were made for the squadron while on R&R in Sydney.
Acknowledgements: Col. Robert Steinkraus USMC(Ret.), Col. Jack Scott USMC(Ret.), Maj. Peter Tonnema USMC(Ret.), Col. J.P. Golden USMC (Ret.)
Manufacturing Details: First issue - Australian embroidered on wool. Second issue - American embroidered on wool.

VMF-123.

Unit: VMF-124

Date Commissioned: 9.7.42

Date Deactivated: 1.31.46

Nickname of Unit: Deathshead Squadron, Checkerboard Squadron

Name of Artist: Red Insignia-Lt. William Crowe
Death's Head Insignia-Lt. William Reynolds
Checkerboard Insignia-Lt. William Reynolds

Date of Insignia: Red Insignia-1943
Death's Head Insignia-late 1943
Checkerboard Insignia-August 1945

Authorization: Red Insignia-local
Death's Head Insignia-HQMC
Checkerboard Insignia-HQMC, disallowed

Type of Aircraft Employed: F4U-1, F3A-1, FG-1, F6F-3

Remarks: The original VMF-124 insignia was designed during the squadron's first overseas combat tour. The numeral "1" over the Marine Corps emblem signifies that VMF-124 was the first Corsair equipped squadron to see combat. Upon its return to the United States Lt. William Crowe asked another squadron member, William Reynolds, to re-design VMF-124's insignia as he felt the original was too general. He wanted something more individual and meaningful for VMF-124. The second insignia retained the Corsair wings, the numeral one, and the oval shape. Instead of a solid red background, a checkerboard was proposed to reflect the squadron's nickname - Checkerboard Squadron. A skull was substituted for the Eagle, Globe, and Anchor. The proposed checkerboard background was discarded and the national insignia, a white star on a blue background, was substituted. The insignia in this form was used thru the second combat tour on board the USS Essex. The squadron again returned to the United States in April 1945 for re-organization and training. Seeking to establish it's own identity for the newly formed squadron, the C.O., Maj. James Johnson directed William Reynolds to design another insignia. This time the new insignia featured a gunsight centered on the Japanese Home Islands against a checkerboard background with the numeral "1" in the center. The request for official approval was disapproved on 6 September 1945. However, by that time the new insignia had been manufactured and distributed to all hands.

Acknowledgements: William Reynolds, Col. Don Hopkins USMC(Ret.), Joseph De Paso, L/Col. Warren Nichols USMC(Ret.), Robert Erskine, Rick French.

Manufacturing Details: Red insignia - Australian embroidered on wool. Death's Head - American embroidered. Checkerboard - American embroidered on twill.

First Design.

Second Design.

Third Design.

VMF-124 BOQ MCAS Mojave, getting ready to move out.

VMF-124 2nd Lt. Jim "Sack Time" Glenn with Maj. Marshall's dog Gumbo.

VMF-124 MCAS Mojave 1944, F4U with squadron checkerboard markings bellied in due to failed hydraulics.

VMF-124 Maj. Joe Quilty wearing G-1 with first issue insignia.

VMF-124 2nd Lt. William Bennewitz wearing G-1 with 2nd issue insignia.

Unit: VMSB/VMTB-131
Date Commissioned: 7.7.41, changed to VMTB 6.1.43
Date Deactivated: 11.16.45
Nickname of Unit: n/a
Name of Artist: Maj. Alvin J. Clark USMC(ret.)
Date of Insignia: 1943
Authorization: local
Type of Aircraft Employed: SB2U-3, TBF-1, TBM-1C
Remarks: An insignia was developed and employed on signs around the squadron area. It was never formally submitted to HQMC for approval or manufactured as a patch for wear on flight clothing. The design featured the devil riding an aerial torpedo signifying the role of the squadron and it's primary weapon. There also exists in HQMC archives artwork depicting a coiled rattlesnake in a diamond which was approved 12 December 1940.
Acknowledgements: Maj. Alvin J. Clark USMC(ret.), Russ Eschenberg

Unit: VMSB/VMTB-132
Date Commissioned: 7.7.41, changed to VMTB 10.14.44
Date Deactivated: 11.9.45
Nickname of Unit: VMSB-none, VMTB-Crying Red Asses
Name of Artist: Cactus insignia-L/Col. John H. Stock USMC(ret.)Monkey being hit by artillery shell-Walt Disney Studios Red Donkey insignia-Capt. Byron M. Rip" Radcliffe
Date of Insignia: Cactus insignia-1942 Monkey being hit by artillery shell- 1944 Red Monkey insignia-1945
Authorization: Cactus insignia-HQMC Red Donkey insignia-local
Type of Aircraft Employed: SBD-1, SBD-3, SBD-4, SBD-5, TBM-3E
Remarks: The first design for the insignia of VMSB-132 was drawn by an unknown newspaper artist in Sydney Australia. It was done from a sketch made on Guadalcanal by John Stock, one of the pilots. The numeral 132 represented the squadron designation. VMSB was not allowed to be used for security reasons. The bomb signified the mission of the squadron. The cactus represented the code name for Guadalcanal. The bulldog with a flight helmet and goggles represented Marine aviators. A very limited number of insignias were manufactured and distributed to flight crew only.

VMSB-132 returned to the United States on 26 October 1943. A request for a new insignia design was made to the Walt Disney Studios. The Disney design was never implemented as the designation of the squadron changed to VMTB, reflecting a change of mission and aircraft to torpedo bombing on 14 October 1944. An insignia for VMTB-132 was designed aboard CVE-109 (Cape Gloucester). The red donkey with the blue tears running down its cheeks represented the squadron nickname-"Crying Red Asses". "Red Assed" is a term which was used in the Marine Corps to describe an individual's current status within the Marine Corps.

VMTB-131's skipper, Maj. George Dooley, standing below squadron insignia, designer of insigne Alvin J. Clark with pipe at right of photo.

VMSB-132.

VMSB/VMTB-132 Squadron personnel with "Crying Red Ass" patch on G-1 Jackets.

VMTB-132.

The following excerpt from a letter by the artist gives the background to the circumstances concerning the choice of symbols: "The meaning [of the red donkey] is well known. It not only cleared the immediate brass, who were as steamed about a second tour so late, when we had all had enough because they were there in the Solomons with us. Our skipper, Major Hank Hise had been the skipper of 232 in the islands and did an extra tour there of his own choosing. The rest of us senior officers in 132 had been in 233 and other squadrons that had taken a pounding. As you know, pilots were shifted around into different squadrons in the islands. I was in three of them but spent the greatest time in 233, so relate to that number most easily. When we finally were relieved and sent stateside, most of us did not expect an overseas assignment -at least so soon. After my leave time my orders said Santa Barbara as did those of other good friends of past action. When we all met at Santa Barbara and learned that we were to be a carrier squadron and get shipped out fairly soon, there was a bunch of bitching, naturally. In fact, my stay in the states was only 6 months - and most of that was squadron retraining for carrier operation. In April of '45 we were ready and the ship had completed shakedown - so we went aboard. In May we left for Pearl Harbor after a hectic schedule of carrier operation familiarization. We then left Pearl heading for the China Sea 3 weeks later after more operations - during which 2 of our fighters were lost on night landings operation. So, with the war over in Europe and the Army letting people out on a point system, we were heading back for trouble. The Navy did not have a "point" system until before we were leaving Pearl and the Marine Corps later than that. Each was tougher than that of the Army - ours was the worst. Still, there were many of us who were eligible until an order came down that the "point" system did not apply to those heading out of Pearl. Combining all these factors, the red-ass was a common malady. Just when we adopted the patch, which I drew up in Santa Barbara before shipping out, is uncertain - but we had it in Pearl. Not all the pilots of 132 were shot-up vets, but a good share of us were. Col. Yost, of the fighter squadron (VMF-351) was also boss of both squadrons (in the air group) and had a fine sense of humor plus friends upstairs. He endorsed the patch and we had no problems at all. In fact, the patch got approved faster than any I had ever known of before. I believe that had something to do with making sure we had it as we headed out. Perhaps as pacifier of sorts. Being eligible for release but heading out for action again was the "frosting on the cake."

Acknowledgements: Capt. L. Noble USMC(ret.), L/Col John H. Stock USMC(ret.), Col. John McEniry USMC(ret.), Taylor Roberts, L/Col. John Skinner USMC(ret.), B/Gen. Henry Hise USMC(ret.), Byron M. "Rip" Radcliffe, Mathiew Huminsky, William Lares.

Manufacturing Details: Cactus - Australian embroidered on wool. First issue Crying Red Ass - American chenille. Second issue Crying Red Ass American embroidered on wool.

Proposed Disney design for VMSB/VMTB-132.

Unit: VMSB-133
Date Commissioned: 5.1.43
Date Deactivated: 8.1.45
Nickname of Unit: Flying Eggbeaters
Name of Artist: Concept by Cpl. Andrew Clements, Artwork by Walt Disney Studios.
Date of Insignia: August 1943
Authorization: HQMC
Type of Aircraft Employed: SBD-5, SBD-6
Remarks: The choice of symbols in the insignia of VMSB-133 reflects the squadron's mission of scouting and bombing.
Acknowledgements: Hobart Huff, Howard Ford, Keeling H. "Gunner Jake" Jacobs.
Manufacturing Details: Decal on leather.

VMSB-133.

VMSB/VMTB-134 Tsing Tao China 1945, VMTB-134 signboard with "Dragon" insignia. First four pilots to right of sign are wearing insignia on flight jackets.

Tsing Tao China 1945, VMTB-134.

Unit: VMSB/VMTB-134

Date Commissioned: 6.1.43, changed to VMTB 6.1.43

Date Deactivated: 4.30.46

Nickname of Unit: Rockettes

Name of Artist: TBF/TBM insignia-1st. Lt. Arnold Nodiff China Dragon insignia-n/a

Date of Insignia: TBF/TBM insignia-1943 China Dragon insignia-1945

Authorization: TBF/TBM insignia-HQMC China Dragon insignia-local

Type of Aircraft Employed: SBD-3, TBF-1, TBF-1C, TBM-1C, TBM-3, TBM-3E

Remarks: The squadron nickname was chosen after the squadron gained the distinction of carrying out the first combat test of airborne forward firing rockets in an attack against Japanese in Keravia Bay, Rabaul, New Britain which took place on 17 February 1944. The squadron changed it's insignia when it deployed to Tsingtao China in October 1945.

Acknowledgements: L/Col. Allen O. Hunt USMC (ret.), James S. Conrado Jr.

Manufacturing Details: Decal on leather. No data on any Dragon insignia.

VMTB-134 Patch

VMTB-134 Decal

Unit: VMSB/VMBF/VMTB-141
Date Commissioned: 3.1.42, changed to VMBF 10.14.44, changed to VMSB 12.30.44, changed to VMTB 5.15.45
Date Deactivated: 9.10.45
Nickname of Unit: n/a
Name of Artist: T/Sgt Rodney C. Anderson
Date of Insignia: 1944
Authorization: HQMC
Type of Aircraft Employed: SBD-1, SBD-3, SBD-4, SBD-5, TBM-3E
Remarks: none
Acknowledgements: Rodney C. Anderson, Ken Yonkers, Guy Wirick
Manufacturing Details: American embroidered on twill.

VMSB-141.

Sgt. Rodney Anderson wearing insignia he designed on his flight jacket.

Unit: VMSB-142
Date Commissioned: 3.1.42
Date Deactivated: 9.21.45
Nickname of Unit: n/a
Name of Artist: Lt. Austin Wiggens
Date of Insignia: 1942
Authorization: HQMC
Type of Aircraft Employed: SBD-1, SBD-4, SBD-4P, SBD-5, SBD-6
Remarks: The original insignia carried the words "Tokio Bound" on the bomb being ridden by Bugs Bunny. This was changed to "snafu" when word of Japanese attrocities started to become common knowledge. Flight personnel did not want to provoke the Japanese to additional brutality in the event of capture. "Snafu" was chosen to signify the fact that the squadron was stationed on Emirau from September 1943 to January 1945. There was a distinct feeling that someone had forgotten them.
Acknowledgements: B/Gen. R.B. Conley USMC(ret.), Austin Wiggens, L/Col. Hoyle Barr USMC (ret.), John "Mickey" Cool
Manufacturing Details: Tokio Bound - Australian embroidered on wool. Snafu - American chain stitch embroidery on layers of wool.

VMSB-142, first design.

VMSB-142, second design

VMSB/VMTB-143, first design.

VMSB//VMTB-143, second design.

Unit: VMSB/VMTB-143
Date Commissioned: 9.7.42, changed to VMTB 6.1.43
Date Deactivated: 3.10.46
Nickname of Unit:
> VMSB circa 1943-Devildog Avengers
> VMTB circa 1945-Rocket Raiders

Name of Artist:
> Bulldog riding a torpedo insignia-Philip Miller
> Flash Gordon insignia-Lt. Alex Raymond

Date of Insignia:
> Bulldog riding a torpedo insignia-1943
> Flash Gordon insignia-1945

Authorization:
> Bulldog riding a torpedo insignia-HQMC
> Flash Gordon insignia-local

Type of Aircraft Employed: TBF-1, TBM-3

Remarks: Originally commissioned as a VMSB squadron the designation and mission was changed in mid 1943 to VMTB. The insignia showing a bulldog riding a torpedo reflects the torpedo bomber mission. VMTB 143 returned to the United States in June 1944 for re-training and re-organizationas a carrier squadron. On 12 April 1945 the squadron went aboard the escort carrier USS Gilbert Islands and departed for participation in the Okinawa campaign. While on board the carrier a member of the Marine Corps combat art program, Lt. Alex Raymond who drew the Flash Gordon comic strip in civilian life, designed a new insignia for the squadron. It showed Flash Gordon standing on a HVAR rocket signifying the squadron's change in mission and ordinance, from torpedo bombing to ground support. The artwork was sent back to the United States where cloth insignia were manufactured. The patches were returned in time to be distributed to squadron flight personnel aboard the USS Gilbert Islands.

Acknowledgements: Maj. George B. Woodbury USMC (ret.), L/Col. William Campbell Jr. USMC, B/Gen. Henry Hise USMC (ret.), Philip Miller, Carl Crumpton, James Mitchell, A.E. Seamands, G.P. Adams, Robert Cardino, Con Ward

Manufacturing Details: Bulldog Riding A Torpedo - American embroidered on wool. Flash Gordon - American embroidered on wool.

VMTB-143 aircrew on Bougainville.

VMTB-143 — Aboard CVE 107 Gilbert Islands, Standing L-R Sgt. Philip Miller air gunner, 1st Lt. Rodney P. Johnson F4U pilot, Maj. Elton Mueller XO & pilot wearing VMF-512 insigne, Maj. Blaine H. Baesler CO & pilot, 2nd Lt. Francis L. McCaul TBM pilot wearing VMTB 143 first issue insigne, MTSgt Stanley Groth acting S/Maj VMF-512.

VMSB/VMTB-144, first design.

VMSB/VMTB-144, second design.

Unit: VMSB/VMTB-144

Date Commissioned: 9.7.42, changed to VMTB 10.14.44

Date Deactivated: 12.9.45

Nickname of Unit: Hensagliska Squadron

Name of Artist: Gordon Baldwin

Date of Insignia: 1943

Authorization: HQMC

Type of Aircraft Employed: SBD-3, SBD-4, SB2C-1A, SBD-6, TBM-3E

Remarks: The word "Hensagliska" is a Sioux indian word which when literally translated means "little warrior-brave warrior". It was suggested for inclusion into the design by Reynolds "Chief" Moody, one or the squadron pilots. A patch was manufactured in Sydney Australia during an R&R and issued to flight personnel only as the ground echelon was not stationed with the flight echelon. It was held at Efate and employed as a service and maintenance squadron while the flight echelon flew combat sorties from Guadalcanal and did not participate in the original distribution of insignia The entire squadron was reunited and returned to the United States in January 1944 for re-organization and retraining. It was during this period in 1944 that the original design was modified and manufactured as an insignia which was issued to all personnel. In the modified design, the background was changed to light blue, the numeral "144" was deleted for security reasons as was the "daisy -cutter" fuse.

Acknowledgements: L/Col. Reynolds "Chief" Moody USMC(ret.), Seeley Major, Jack Dwyer III, John Hederman, C.C. Peterson, Gordon Baldwin, L/Col. Saul Millstein USMC(ret.), L/Col. Frank Simonds USMC (ret.)..

Manufacturing Details: First issue - Australian embroidered on wool. Second issue - decal on leather.

VMSB-144 Guadalcanal 1943. Living quarters for flight personnel.

VMTB-144 Henderson Field, Guadalcanal, February 5, 1943. VMSB-144 pilots and gunners shortly after arriving by SCAT R4D ferry flight. Seated L-R, Unidentified, 1st Lt. George "Buck" Brown, 1st Lt. Dan O. Jones, Unidentified, Unidentified, Capt. Edward Ochoa, T/Sgt. Eldon "Bud" Ballard.

VMSB-144 Efate January 1943, VMSB-144 pilots. L-R 1st Lt. Harry J. "Andy" Anderson, 1st Lt. Coot H. Nelson, 1st Lt. Warren D. Brainard, 1st Lt. Hershel S. Carver, 1st Lt. Fred Gilhuly.

VMTB-144 Guadalcanal 1943. 1st Lt. George "Buck" Brown in the sandbagged tent area.

The Pilots Card Game. It began on Guadalcanal and stayed with the squadron until it returned to the States in early 1944. Aircrew and military personnel transiting through were always invited to partake of the squadron's hospitality. Capt. Frank Simonds was able to pay off the mortgage on his mother's house by the end of the three combat tours. Seated l-r Capt. Ollie Greene, Capt. Frank Simonds, 1st Lt. Robert Carr, Capt. Edward Ochoa, unknown, 1st Lt. Coot H. Nelson.

VMSB-144 — Standing L-R Capt. John Kuhn, Capt. William D. Regan, Capt. Frank Simonds.

Russel Islands, 1943 - Pilots and Gunners of VMSB-144 L-R Back row: unkown, Frank Taylor, Ed Ochoa, Reynolds "Chief" Moody, unkown, Ken Chamberlain, Roscoe Nelson, Jim Dougherty, Doc Shellman, unknown, Abe "Danny" Daniels, "Coot" Nelson, Bob Brumley, Frank Simons, unknown, Tholo johnson, Willie Regan. Front row: Buck Brown, Perry Aliff, Saul "Millie" Millstein (behind Perry), Harry "Andy" Anderson, Harold "HF" Brown, unkown, P.J. Carmichael

VMSB-144 — Guadalcanal, 1943. L-R Pilots Bill Regan and Ollie Greene. "Peaceful Valley. Formerly Bloody Gulch. No Bombing, strafing, or shelling permitted by Axis rats."

VMSB-144 — Russel Islands, 1943. Capt. Perry Aliffe standing on the wing of his SBD, the 3 Japanese battle flags next to the radio mast for hits of Jap shipping.

Unit: VMO/VMTB/VMSB-151

Date Commissioned: 7.7.41, changed to VMSB 9.15.42, changed to VMTB 6.30.45

Date Deactivated: 3.20.46

Nickname of Unit: Ali Baba Squadron

Name of Artist: n/a

Date of Insignia: 1943

Authorization: HQMC

Type of Aircraft Employed: SBC-4, J2F-5, SBD-4, SBD-5

Remarks: none

Acknowledgements: L/Col. John Stock USMC(ret.), Col. Randolph Berkeley USMC(ret.), Col. Robert Zitnik USMC(ret.), L/Col. Charles Quinn USMC (ret.)

VMSB-151.

Unit: VMJ/VMR-152

Date Commissioned: 7.7.41, changed to VMR 6.3.44

Date Deactivated: n/a

Nickname of Unit: n/a

Name of Artist: n/a

Date of Insignia: n/a

Authorization: n/a

Type of Aircraft Employed: R4D-1, R4D-5

Remarks: Used the insignia of MAG-25 also known as "SCAT". See Mag-25.

Acknowledgements: none

VMSB-151 sign with squadron designation taped out as per Group orders.

Unit: VMJ/VMR-153

Date Commissioned: 3.1.42, changed to VMR 6.3.44

Date Deactivated:

Nickname of Unit: n/a

Name of Artist: n/a

Date of Insignia: n/a

Authorization: n/a

Type of Aircraft Employed: R4D-1, JO-2, J2F-5, R4D-5, R5O-4

Remarks: Used the insignia of MAG-25 also known as "SCAT". See MAG-25.

Acknowledgements: none

VMD-154 — Warren Swanson, designer of the VMD-154 insignia, standing extreme right. Note two victory flags below pilot compartment side window.

VMD-1.

VMD-154.

VMO-155.

Unit: VMD-1, VMD-154
Date Commissioned: 4.1.42, changed to VMD-154
9.15.42
Date Deactivated: 9.10.45
Nickname of Unit:
VMD-1 n/a
VMD-154 The Pathfinders
Name of Artist:
VMD-1 n/a
VMD-154 S/Sgt. Warren Swanson
Date of Insignia:
VMD-1 1942
VMD-154 1943
Authorization:
VMD-1 local
VMD-154 HQMC
Type of Aircraft Employed:
VMD-1 SNJ-3, J2F-5.
VMD-154 F4F-7, PB4Y-1, SNJ-4, F6F-3,
F6F-3P
Remarks: none
Acknowledgements: Warren Swanson, Irving Hirst,
J.F. Lisiky, Ernest Haff, Dallas Willis, Roger
Rowland.
Manufacturing Details: VMD-1 American embroi-
dered on wool. VMD-154 American embroidered
on twill.

Unit: VMO/VMF-155
Date Commissioned: 10.1.42, changed to VMF
1.31.45
Date Deactivated: 10.15.45
Nickname of Unit: Ready Teddys
Name of Artist: Mrs. J.R. Thayer
Date of Insignia: 1944
Authorization: HQMC
Type of Aircraft Employed: F4F-3, F4F-3A, F4F-3P,
F4F-4, F4F-7, OS2U-3, SNJ-4, F4U-1, F4U-1D,
SBD-6
Remarks: "As for Ready Teddy, he was a comic char-
acter of the forties and someone suggested it as a
patch. My wife, who is a profesional artist, was
asked if she could draw a bear who looked like a
pilot so a jacket patch could be made. She did
and the patches were made in San Diego and worn
on flight jackets." Excerpted from a letter dated
1.29.92
Acknowledgements: Lt. Col. J.R. Thayer USMCR
(ret.), Edgar Dies
Manufacturing Details: Decal on leather.

Christmas card sent home from Majuro Island, 1944.

Unit: VMF-211

Date Commissioned: 6.28.41, changed to VMA 6.30.52

Date Deactivated: still active

Nickname of Unit: Wake Avengers

Name of Artist: Maj. Charles Endweiss

Date of Insignia: 1943

Authorization: HQMC

Type of Aircraft Employed: F2A-3, SNJ-4, F4F, F4U-1, F4U-1D

Remarks: VMF-211 traced it's lineage back to the pre-war VMF-2 (Fighting Two). The leaping red lion of the original VMF-2 insignia was placed between the horns of the Wake Island atoll by Maj. Charles Endweiss in tribute to friends and fellow fliers who were either killed or captured in the defense of Wake. It was also at this time that the backgroumd color was changed from green to white.

Acknowledgements: Col. Thomas V. Murto USMC(ret.), Col. Charles G.Carr USMC(ret.), Ray Foust, Jr.

Manufacturing Details: VMF-211 Australian embroidered on wool. Embroidered on silk in China .

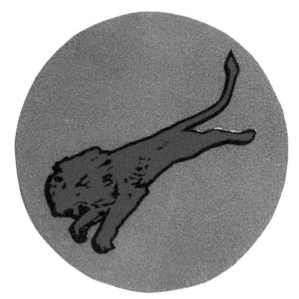

VMF-2.

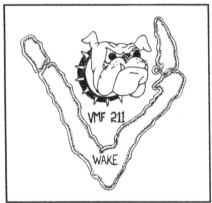

Proposed design for VMF-211.

VMF-211.

Unit: VMF-212

Date Commissioned: 3.1.42, changed to VMA 6.10.52, to VMF 7.1.63, to VMF(AW) 7.1.64, to VMF 3.1.68, to VMFA 8.10.68

Date Deactivated: still active

Nickname of Unit:
Early war-none
Late war-Musketeers

Name of Artist:
Bulldog with Tommygun insignia-Walt Disney Studios
Musketeer insignia-n/a

Date of Insignia:
Bulldog with Tommygun insignia-1942
Musketeer insignia-6.6.45

Authorization: Both insignia were approved by HQMC.

Type of Aircraft Employed: F4F-3A, J2F-5, SNJ-3, F4F-3, F4F-4, FM-1, F4U-1, F4U-4

Remarks: VMF-212 used the Disney insignia until the late spring of 1945 when the "Musketeers" insignia was approved for use. The significance of the new insignia was derived from the military discipline, loyalty, and teamwork displayed by the Musketeers in the written works of Dumas.

VMF-212.

VMF-212 score board.

Acknowledgements: Col. J.P. McMahon USMC(ret.), William N. Payne, Dr. Walter Tucker, James T. Sykes, Col. James K. Dill USMC(ret.), B/Gen. Frederick R. Payne USMC(ret.), Col. Loren B. Everton USMC(ret.), Philip C. Beals, William Nickerson, Maj. John M. Elliott USMC(ret.)

Manufacturing Details: Australian embroidered on wool.

Proposed art for VMF-212.

VMF-212 — Efate 1942. Capt. Jack Conger flanked by two unidentified enlisted men. Capt. Conger eventually ended the war with 10 victories. His most famous occurred when he used his prop to chew the tail off a Zero after running out of ammunition. Both pilots successfully parachuted from their damaged aircraft. A passing P.T. boat first picked up Capt. Conger from the water and then headed over to the Japanese pilot who was floating nearby. When the Japanese pilot pulled out a pistol and tried to shoot him, a furious Conger subdued him with a boat hook.

VMF-212 — L-R Travers, Bonnett, Brown, Dwyer, Slingerland, Jacobson, Elwood, Niece, Grill. Bonnett, Jacobson, Niece and Grill did not make it home.

VMF-212 — Efate 1942, L-R, F.R. "Fritz" Payne (5 Victories), C.J. "Chick" Quilter (3 Victories). M.M. Martin (Flight Surgeon), H.W. "Joe" Bauer (10 Victories), L.D. "Doc" Everton (10 Victories).

VMF-212 — Guadalcanal 1942, Capt. Loren "Doc" Everton in his F4F-3 Wildcat with the "Fighting Bulldog" insignia painted on the starboard instrument panel access door.

VMF-212 — Efate 1942, L-R Pfc. Vance, S/Sgt. Robertson on the wing of Doc Everton's F4F-3.

VMF-213 — Hellhawks, February 1943.

VMF-213, first design.

Unit: VMF-213
Date Commissioned: 7.1.42
Date Deactivated: 4.24.46
Nickname of Unit: Hellhawks
Name of Artist: n/a
Date of Insignia: 1942
Authorization: HQMC
Type of Aircraft Employed: F4U-1, F3A-1, FG-1, F6F-3, F6F-5, F6F-3P
Remarks: The original design was produced as an patch during an R&R in Sydney Australia. Later in the war a directive came out which banned the use of red as a background color for use in unit insignia on aircraft. The design was changed to a blue background and the motto "Hellhawks Fight" dropped. The modified insignia was used by VMF-213 personnel aboard the USS Essex.
Acknowledgements: Robert Kotzmoyer, Plane Captain "Si" Hewitt, Col. James T. Anderson USMC (ret.)
Manufacturing Details: First issue Australian embroidered on wool. Second issue American embroidered on twill. Essex echelon American embroidered on twill.

VMF-213, second design aboard USS Essex.

Lt. Garrison standing in front of his Corsair which he named "Poncho's Consuelo."

VMF-213 — June 1943. Unidentified enlisted man in front of "Poncho's Consuelo."

VMF-213 — Unidentified enlisted man.

Lt. Foy Garrison credited with the destruction of two Zeros over Kahili on June 30th, 1943, during the squadron's second combat tour. On 17 July 1943, according to VMF-213's war diary, the squadron was bounced by 20-30 Zeros over Rendova Island. Four Zeros attacked Lt. Garrison from behind, out of the sun, and Lt. Garrison was last seen diving in flames towards the water.

VMF-213 — Robert Kotzmoyer.

VMF-213 — Officer's Club.

VMF-213 — June 1943. Lt. Foy Garrison's crew on the wing of "Poncho's Consuelo."

VMF-213 — Hell Hawks tally board in front of operations tent.

First Tour.

VMF-214 — Lt. David W. Rankin wearing "Swashbucklers" insignia.

Unit: VMF-214

Date Commissioned: 7.1.42, changed to VMF(AW) 12.31.56, to VMA 7.9.57

Date Deactivated: still active

Nickname of Unit:
First two combat tours-Swashbucklers
With Maj. Boyington as C.O.-Blacksheep

Name of Artist:
Swashbucklers insignia-Lt. Harry Hollmeyer
Blacksheep insignia-Pen Johnson

Date of Insignia:
Swashbucklers insignia-August 1943
Blacksheep insignia-late 1943

Authorization:
Swashbucklers insignia-local
Blacksheep insignia-HQMC

Type of Aircraft Employed: FG-1, SB2C-4E

Remarks: VMF-214 began combat operations on 15 March 1943. After completing their first combat tour the squadron to the main base in the New Hebrides for retraining and transition to F4U Corsairs. One of the squadron members, Lt. Harry Hollmeyer, noticed that a lot of the squadrons sharing the base had their own insignia. "I began thinking that we should have our own also. We were starting to fly Corsairs-Corsairs were pirates - SWASHBUCKLERS were pirates. Their flag was the skull and crossbones. Use the bent wings of the Corsair instead of crossbones - banked, with the skull instead of the cowling-scare the hell out of Jap pilots.....Next a Latin motto - I knew as a longtime aviation buff that RAF squadrons had them. The Marines had "Semper Fidelis". So the start was made, and became "Semper Vincere" - "Always To Conquer". I thought it was a great sequitur, both to the Marines and to the RAF tradition. The other squadrons had arranged to get their patches in Sydney and I was able to do the same when we went down there for our second leave (of one week and an extra day). No idea of the cost but suppose that it might have been $100 for 30 patches-$200 at most for 50. Thinking it over, everything happened too rapidly - as far as I know, no one ever gave approval, officially or otherwise. Our VMF-214 was divided up for our last tour, which we all thought was not correct. But as a friend said later "Sic transit gloria Munda"."

Upon return to Espiritu Santo for a third combat tour, the squadron was disbanded with some pilots being returned to the United States and others being transferred to other squadrons as replacements. The squadron's numerical designation was reassigned to Maj. Gregory Boyington where it became the "Blacksheep". Aside from the official Blacksheep insignia there also exists a piece of artwork done by the Walt Disney Studios for a proposed insignia which was never used.

Acknowledgements: Col. Donald Fisher USMC(ret.), Maj. Edwin Olander USMC(ret.), Dr. William Hunter, Col. Frank E. Walton USMC(ret.), L/Col. Keith Williams USMC(ret.), David Rankin, Harry Hollmeyer

Manufacturing Details: Swashbucklers - Australian embroidered on wool. First issue Blacksheep - Australian embroidered on wool. Second issue Blacksheep - American embroidered on wool.

VMF-214 — Maj. Gregory Boyington with 20 victory flags painted on "Lucybelle."

Worn on board USS Franklin.

Unit: VMF-215

Date Commissioned: VMSB-242 3.1.42, changed to VMF-215 9.15.42

Date Deactivated: 11.13.46

Nickname of Unit: Fightin' Corsairs

Name of Artist: n/a

Date of Insignia: 1943

Authorization: HQMC

Type of Aircraft Employed: F4U-1, SNJ-4, F4U-1D, FG-1, FG-1D, F6F-5, F6F-5P

Remarks: none

Acknowledgements: L/Col. Harold Langstaff USMC(ret.), Gene Musinski, Larry Smith

Manufacturing Details: American embroidered on wool.

VMF-215.

VMF-216 Bull Dogs.

Unit: VMF-216
Date Commissioned: 1.1.43
Date Deactivated: 3.10.45
Nickname of Unit: Bull Dogs
Name of Artist: Lt. Charles Schwartz
Date of Insignia: 1943
Authorization: local
Type of Aircraft Employed: F4F-4, F4U-1, SNJ-3, F6F-3, F6F-5
Remarks: none
Acknowledgements: L/Col. Roland E. Marker USMC(ret.), Lowell Wilkerson, Ben Hargrave, Jim Anderson.

VMF-217.

Unit: VMF-217
Date Commissioned: 9.15.43 Deactivated: 3.10.46
Nickname of Unit: Max's Wild Hares
Name of Artist: concept by Maj. Howard Meyer USMC(ret.)
Date of Insignia: 1943
Authorization: HQMC
Type of Aircraft Employed: F4U-1, F6F-5E
Remarks: "While Marine Fighting Squafron 217 was forming at El Centro,California (in 1943) it was my drawing that was selected as the squadron logo. This drawing was then taken by Lt. J.E.P. Mogan to the Disney Studios. Since it depicted a rabbit as it's main character, the Disney Studio wouldn't do anything with it. Instead, they drew up a beautiful insignia showing a Marine Corps Bulldog in the ring. The sketch was then taken to Leon Schlesinger Studio and it was Leon Schlesinger who did the accepted rendition using Bugs Bunny. Thus the official insignia (in black and white) bears the inscription "copyright on Schlesinger". It was sometime later that the squadron picked up the nickname Max's Wild Hares-Max being Major Max Read- Skipper." Excerpt from a letter by Maj. Howard Mayer USMC(ret.) dated 7.22.85
Acknowledgements: B.B. Turnage, Maj. Howard Meyer USMC(ret.), Michael R. Mulligan, Jack B. Quisenberry.
Manufacturing Details: American fully embroidered.

Unit: VMF-218
Date Commissioned: 9.15.43
Date Deactivated: 12.31.49
Nickname of Unit: Hellions
Name of Artist:
Lion insignia-Sgt. George Hughes
Dragon insignia-Lt. Dean Dirkson
Date of Insignia:
Lion insignia-1944
Dragon insignia-1946
Authorization:
Lion insignia-HQMC
Dragon insignia-HQMC, disapproved
Type of Aircraft Employed: F4U-1D, FG-1, FG-1D
Remarks: There was no significance to the symbols used in the "Lion" insignia. Members of the squadron were invited to submit sketches and this particular design was selected strictly on the esthetics. In the spring of 1946, while the squadron was deployed in China, a new design symbollically closer to the squadron's role was drawn by Lt. Dean Dirkson. The design, the world in the clutches of a dragon with a Corsair flying through the center, was submitted to HQMC for approval. The new design was disapproved on the basis that the function of the unit and the aircraft employed had not changed. The new insignia was produced as a patch and worn by squadron personnel while in China.
Acknowledgements: Robert A. Enders, Chuck Barton, Bruce Singleton, Earl W. McCabe, L/Col. Robert Kingsbury USMC(ret.), C.E. Corley, Roger Ervin, L/Col. A.J. Baretsky USMC(ret.).
Manufacturing Details: Lion - American embroidered on wool. Dragon - embroidered on silk in China.

VMF-218, First Design.

VMF-218, Second Design.

VMF-218-- Lt. Dean F. Dirkson at work designing "Hellions" insignia.

VMF-218--Capt. Oscar Bate, operations officer.

VMF-221 insignia.

Unit: VMF-221
Date Commissioned: 7.11.41
Date Deactivated: 9.10.45
Nickname of Unit: Fighting Falcons
Name of Artist: Lt. Harold "Manny" Segal
Date of Insignia: 1943
Authorization: HQMC
Type of Aircraft Employed: F2A-3, F4F-3, F4F-4,
    SNJ-4, F3A-1, FG-1, F4U-1, SB2C-4E
Remarks: none
Acknowledgements: Col. James Swett USMC(ret.),
    Blaine Imel, Charles Nettles.
Manufacturing Details: American embroidered on
    wool.

Above: Victory flag decal.

Left: VMF-221 Squadron Roster with insignia.

V.M.F. 221
Fighting Falcons

MAJOR NATHAN T. POST Jr.- COMMANDING OFFICER

MAJORS	1st. LIEUTENANTS	2nd LIEUTENANTS
EDWIN S. ROBERTS Jr.	ROBERT H. BENTLEY	WILLIAM L. BAILEY
ROBLEY E. WEST	JOSEPH BROCIA Jr.	FREDERICK E. BRIGGS
	JARVIS H. CARPENTER	EUGENE D. CAMERON
CAPTAINS	CHARLES R. DENISON	DEAN CASWELL
WILLIAM ALEXANDER	FRANK E. FRISK	WALTER GOEGGEL Jr.
DONALD L. BALCH	RALPH O. GLENDINNING	WILLIAM M. HUFF
FRANK B. BALDWIN	CLAY D. HAGGARD	GEORGE R. JOHNS
JOHN B. DELANCEY	ARTHUR B. IMEL Jr.	DONALD G. MAC FARLANE
WILLIAM N. SNIDER	JOHN E. JORGENSON	JAMES MC KENZIE
JAMES E. SWETT	ADOLPH J. KISSELL Jr.	DAVID G. NICHOLS
	EARL W. LANGSTON	EDWARD K. NICOLAIDES
	ROBERT J. MURRAY	WILLIAM R. ORMES
	CHARLES M. NETTLES	WILLIAM M. PEMBLE
	"C"."B" QUICK	GEORGE REICHGOTT
	KENNETH S. ROSS	LEONARD SALIT
	GERALD D. SCOTT	NORMAN E. SARK
MEDICAL OFFICERS	NORMAN D. SMITH	RICHARD SHASSERRE
LT. DONALD G. PIKE		ROBERT J. TESTO
		RICHARD WASLEY

Unit: VMF-222

Date Commissioned: 3.1.42

Date Deactivated: 12.31.49

Nickname of Unit: Flying Deuces, SeaBee Air Force

Name of Artist: Gunner George Schaeffer

Date of Insignia: 1942

Authorization: in use at the local level, submitted to HQMC for approval February 1945, approved 28 February 1947.

Type of Aircraft Employed: F2A-2, F2A-3, F4F-3A, SNJ-3, F4U-1, F4U-4

Remarks: The original insignia employed by the squadron was on a greendisc with the word "FLYING" above the playing cards and the word "DEUCES" below them. A U.S. manufactured version was produced which was no longer a disc, just the winged playing cards in front of the red vee, and meant for wear on caps.

"VMF-222 acquired its unique title 'SeaBee Air Force' as a result of the conditions which this squadron encountered upon arrival in the Phillippines. The 83rd and 61st CB Battalions were on the site, constructing the airstrip and other facilities. Every unit ordered into Guiuan was literally in the process of stamping something out of the ground. Of these days the first few are the worst, for almost nothing is established; food facilities, transportation, tentage, water, operating space and facilities, all are touch and go at first. At such times a helping hand from someone already established is most appreciated, and the CBs were just the people to lend a hand when most needed. Marine relations with the SeaBees have always been good. In the Phillippines it became a model of interservice regard and esteem between VMF-222 and the 61st CB Battalion. Friendships sprang up which are remembered with pleasure even to this day. Accordingly when one of my top NCOs came to me one day with a CB friend of his, suggesting that we carry the CB insignia on our airplanes, the idea was accepted with enthusiasm on my part, and I gave them the go-ahead, subject to the approval by the Commander of the 61st CBs. This was quickly granted, and the "SeaBee Air Force" was born. As each of our Corsairs came in for a routine check the cowling was taken off and driven to the 61st CB paint shop, where the CB insignia was promptly painted on and the cowling returned to us for reinstallation, VMF-122 carried this large insignia all over the Phillippines, from Mindanao to Luzon, as a singular mark of respect for a great organization." (excerpted from letter by Col. Roy T. Spurlock USMCR(ret.) dated 6 November 1985).

Acknowledgements: Col. Robert Foxworth USMC(ret.), Col. Roy T. Spurlock USMCR(ret.), John Nugent, B/Gen Max Volcansek USMC(ret.), Gunner George Schaeffer, Col. Wesley Hazlett USMC(ret.), Col. John Foster USMC(ret.), Col. Robert W. Wilson USMC(ret.)

Manufacturing Details: first issue - Australian embroidered on wool. Second issue - American embroidered on twill.

VMF-222, First design.

VMF-222, Second design used as cap insignias.

VMF-222 — Midway 1943 - The raising of the squadron flag, Cpl. Hartman kneeling, Major Max Volcansac sitting, unidentified standing.

VMF-222 — *Midway 1943 - Pilot Jack Foster standing on wing of F4U "Linda II," plane crew standing along side of wing. Man at left wears baseball hat with cap insignia;*

VMF-222 — *Midway 1943 - Pilot Don Stapp (11 victories) standing on wing of F4U "Blue Phantom," plane crew in front of wing.*

VMF-222 — *F4U "Mary Jo" with Pilot H.M. "Bud" Turner on wing.*

VMF-222 — "Bud" Turner and "Mary Jo."

Spring 1945 - VMF-222 aircraft with the "CB Airforce" insignia painted on the cowl. Pilots "Bob" Dugan and "Dumbo" Graham with 61st CB personnel.

VMF-222 — Midway 1943 - Pilot W.O. Reid on wing on F4U "Arkansas Traveler."

VMF-222 — W.O. Reid and plane crew.

William D. "Willie" Moore, last seen diving into a group of enemy fighters off Munda September 1943. Never seen again.

Richard L. "Kitty" Hobbs.

Marine Gunner George C. Schaeffer, the amateur photographer who photographs chronicle the history of VMF-222.

VMF-222 taking possession of one of it's first F4Us at Santa Barbara, late 1942.

MCAS Santa Barbara late 1942 - Major Max Volcansac (C.O. of VMF-222 from 28 September 1942 to 4 November 1943) and W.O. Reid with helmets and goggles deliver the squadron's first two F4U aircraft by flying them in from San Diego.

Midway 1943 - F4U "Dynamite."

Midway 1943 - F4U Dynamite.

MCAS Santa Barbara late 1942 - Pilot W.O. Reid and one of the first two F4Us.

L-R Major Roy Spurlock (C.O. of VMF-222 from 6 April 1944 to 27 April 1945), Col. Charles Lindburgh, Capt. Johnson (pilot) during Lindberg's visit to train pilots how to extend the effective range of single engine fighter aircraft.

Just before going home, "Ace" Newlands, "Pappy" Reid, "Okie" McLean, "Hooter" Stapp. No one needed to tell them to smile for the camera.

One of VMF-222's replacement aircraft still wearing VMF-115 squadron insignia.

Lt. Peru standing on the wing of one of the ex-VMF 115 aircraft assigned to VMF-222 with the 115 insigne still visable.

Midway 1943 - Richard L. "Kitty" Hobbs, Squadron entrepenneur.

Major Max Volcansac displaying squadron flag.

"The shot in the ass with luck" club. Membership open to any pilot who had gotten a bullet hole in his aircraft. Standing L-R Hazlett, Williams, Carnagey, McLean, Hughes (the president by virtue of being the worst shot up), Craig, Morris, Reid. Kneeling L-R Koetsch, Volcansak, Gordon, Gher, Moore.

Kneeling L-R Nugent, Perino, Hazlett (wearing baseball hat with cap insignia), Koetsch. Standing L-R Mack, McLean, Newlands, Langley, Witt, Carrell.

Unit: VMF-223
Date Commissioned: 5.1.42, changed to VMA 12.1.54
Date Deactivated: still active
Nickname of Unit: Rainbow Squadron
Name of Artist: Walt Disney Studios
Date of Insignia: 12 April 1943
Authorization: HQMC
Type of Aircraft Employed: F2A-3, SNJ-3, SNJ-4, F4F-3, F4F-4, FM-1, F4U-1, F4U-4
Remarks: none
Acknowledgements: Col. Robert Teller USMC(ret.), Paul Steerup, Larry W. DeCamp, Rex Hamilton, James T. Sykes, Jene Ukena.
Manufacturing Details: Australian embroidered on wool.

VMF-223.

L-R Pilots Perry Lane, Bill Andreae (wearing squadron insignia on flight clothing), unidentified, John Morgan.

Quoin Hill New Hibrides, November 1943. Rex Hamilton went to Guadalcanal as a seventeen year old.

The Pagoda at Henderson Field, Guadalcanal 1942.

Marion E. Carl, 18.5 victories, kneeling next to squadron tally board.

L-R Pilots Scott Gier, Wallace Henry, William Shanks, James Sykes (wearing squadron insignia on summer flying jacket).

VMF-224.

Unit: VMF-224
Date Commissioned: 5.1.42, changed to VMA 12.1.54
Date Deactivated: still active
Nickname of Unit: Fighting Wildcats
Name of Artist: Walt Disney Studios
Date of Insignia: 12 April 1943
Authorization: HQMC
Type of Aircraft Employed: F2A-3, F4F, F4U-1,
    F4U-1D, FG-1D
Remarks: none
Acknowledgements: Col. Howard A. "Rudy" York
    USMC (ret.), John A Hughes, Col. Reynolds
    "Chief" Moody USMC (ret.).
Manufacturing Details: American chenille.

VMF-225, First design.

nit: VMF-225
Jate Commissioned: 1.11.43, changed to VMA
    6.17.52
Date Deactivated: still active
Nickname of Unit: n/a
Name of Artist:
    Kangaroo insignia-Walt Disney Studios
    Spade insignia-Lt Jack Butler
Date of Insignia:
    Kangaroo insignia-1943
    Spade insignia-1944
Authorization:
    Kangaroo insignia-local
    Spade insignia-local
Type of Aircraft Employed: F4F-3, F4U-1, SNJ-3,
    SNJ-4
Remarks: While stationed at Mojave, one of the squad-
    ron members wrote to the Walt Disney Studios
    and requested a squadron insignia design. The
    Disney Studios -designed "Kangaroo" emblem
    was discarded as being too cute. In its place the
    design drawn by Lt. Jack Butler became the offi-
    cial squadron logo.
Acknowledgements: George "Joe" Crandall, Robert
    Karcher, Robert Harvey, Olin Wollin.
Manufacturing Details: Kangaroo - silk screened on
    canvas. Spade - decal on leather.

VMF-225, Second design.

Espirito Santos 11944 VMF-225 Ground Crew.
Standing L-R: Red Morris, Gus ?
Kneeling L-R: E.T. Youngblood, Olin Wollen.

Unit: VMSB/VMTB-231

Date Commissioned: 7.15.41, changed to VMTB 8.1.45

Date Deactivated: 3.20.46,
Reactivated: 7.31.73 and changed to VMFA, still active

Nickname of Unit: Ace Of Spades Squadron

Name of Artist: Gen. Hayne Boyden USMC(ret.)

Date of Insignia: 1921

Authorization: HQMC

Type of Aircraft Employed: SBD-1, SBD-3, SBD-4, SBD-5, TBF-1, TBM-1, SBD-6, SB2C-4

Remarks: The Ace of Spades insignia is the first one ever used by a Marine Squadron. It was designed by Gen. Hayne D. Boyden USMC(ret.) early in 1921 and was selected by the judges as the most distinctive of the 350 designs submitted in a contest to choose a motif for an insignia for the First Air Squadron, then in the Dominican Republic. The First Air Squadron was organized from remnants of the First Aviation Force which had served in France and was ordered from Miami, Florida to Santo Domingo in February 1919. Originally the Ace of Spades insignia was designed with an "S " instead of the lower "A", so that as an insignia it would symbolize the First Air Squadron, the ace being the first card of the suit, upper "A" for air and "S" for squadron. The significance of the lower "S" was eventually lost and changed to the lower "A" on the design employed by VMSB/VMTB-231.

Acknowledgements: Col. Elmer Glidden USMC(ret.)

Manufacturing Details: American embroidered on wool.

Unit: VMSB/VMTB-232

Date Commissioned: 7.15.41, changed to VMTB 6.1.43

Date Deactivated: 11.16.45,
Reactivated: 9.18.50, changed to VMF(AW) 3.1.65, to VMFA 9.8.67, still active.

Nickname of Unit: Red Devils

Name of Artist: n/a

Date of Insignia: Red Devil insignia-1920's
Devil Riding A Torpedo insignia-1943

Authorization: Red Devil insignia-HQMC
Devil Riding A Torpedo insignia-local

Type of Aircraft Employed: SBD-2, SBD-3, TBF-1, TBM-1, TBM-3, TBM-3E

Remarks: The insigtne of VMSB/VMTB dates back to the 1920's when the Red Devil was a "Winged Devil" on the aircraft of VF-10M stationed in Tientsin, China. Through time the wings on the Devil evolved to a cape flowing behind a running red Devil. For a short time in 1943, while the squadron flew combat from Guadalcanal and Munda, the Devil rode a torpedo. This design was painted on flight jackets by Lt. Philip St. George-Fields. After 1943 the design reverted to the "Running Red Devil".

Acknowledgements: Carl Crumpton, Col. Rolland Smith USMQ(ret.), George Stamets, Ray Brode.

VMSB/VMTB-231.

VMB-2

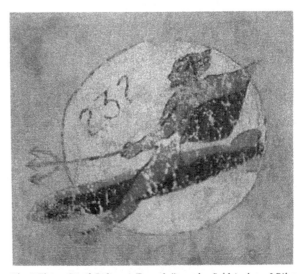

The "Flying Devil Riding A Torpedo" on the field jacket of Pilot George Stamets. The insignia was designed and painted on field jackets and flight gear by Lt. Philip St. George Fields while the squadron was flying from Guadalcanal and Mundal.

Munda 1943 - Several VMTB-232 pilots in front of the Red Devil Squadron tally board.

Col. Richard Mangrum, Marine Dive Bomber Pilot, Guadalcanal.

Closeup of VMSB-233 squadron sign board.

Unit: VMSB/VMTB-233
Date Commissioned: 5.1.42, changed to VMTB 6.13.43
Date Deactivated: 3.10.46
Nickname of Unit: Flying Deadheads
Name of Artist: Ronald Crowell
Date of Insignia: 1944
Authorization: HQMC
Type of Aircraft Employed: TBF-1, TBM-1, TBM-3, TBM-3P
Remarks: none
Acknowledgements: Ted Kruze, W/O Barney Castor USMC (ret.)
Manufacturing Details: American embroidered on wool.

VMSB-233.

Captain Frank Takis at debriefing on the Block Island. Unidentified squadron member wears Flying Deadhead insignia on his G-1 flight jacket

Unit: VMSB/VMTB-234

Date Commissioned: 5.1.42, changed to VMTB 10.14.44

Date Deactivated: 3.20.46

Nickname of Unit: n/a

Name of Artist:
Dropping Bomb insignia-Pfc. Richard Green
Winged Fist insignia-n/a

Date of Insignia: Dropping Bomb insignia-1943
Winged Fist insignia-1944

Authorization: HQMC for both

Type of Aircraft Employed: SBD-1, F4F-3, SBD-3P, SBD-4, SBD-4P, SBD-5, TBM-3E

Remarks: This squadron employed two different insignia. The first depicted a bomb being dropped which signified it's role as a scout bombing squadron. The second showed a mailed fist with a set of Avenger wings signifying the change in mission and aircraft from SBD to TBF/TBM and a change in designation from VMSB to VMTB.

Acknowledgements: L/Col. Robert B. Ayers USMC(ret.), Art Foster, Andrew Foreman.

Manufacturing Details: First issue Dropping Bomb - Australian embroidered on wool. Second issue Dropping Bomb - American fully embroidered. Winged Fist - American fully embroidered.

VMSB-234, First design.

Unit: VMSB-235

Date Commissioned: 1.1.43

Date Deactivated: 11.10.44,

Reactivated: 9.18.50, changed to VMF(AW) 2.1.62, to VMFA 9.30.68

Nickname of Unit: n/a

Name of Artist: Paul Brink

Date of Insignia: 1944

Authorization: local

Type of Aircraft Employed: SBD-5

Remarks: "The insignia in question showed up late in the squadron's overseas tour. As I recall, it was made available to ground echelon personnel while we were on Bougainville which was our last major action. That would put it in the first three months of 1944. It was the final swing of our flight echelon and they brought the insignia to us from Australia where, I understand, they were made. As you probably know, squadron flight echelons rotated between combat & Australia while the ground echelons stayed put and took it on the chin. I always drew a lot of pictures, some of them humerous cartoons of the squadron bungles for the bulletin board, and was sort of the camp artist. A radio-gunner from the flight echelon named Jerry (Jerome) Wander asked me to draw a picture of a wolf riding a bomb which was a concensus choice of the flight echelon to be the squadron insignia. This I believe, happened on Munda prior to our flight echelon leaving us on rotation. I drew it in pencil, having no india ink, and colored it with a set of colored pencils I'd purchased in Honolulu. The vivid colors were added by the manufacturer. Jerry took the drawing with him when the flight echelon departed for Australia and when they rejoined us on Bougainville he had the patches with him. It was largely a flight echelon affair and I don't think too many ground personnel ever got one. Jerry made a point of giving me one for obvious reasons." excerpt from a letter dated 1.23.93

Acknowledgements: Col. Earl B. "Slim" Summerlin USMC (ret.), William P. Toth, Samuel Lichtman, Paul Brink.

Manufacturing Details: Australian embroidered on wool.

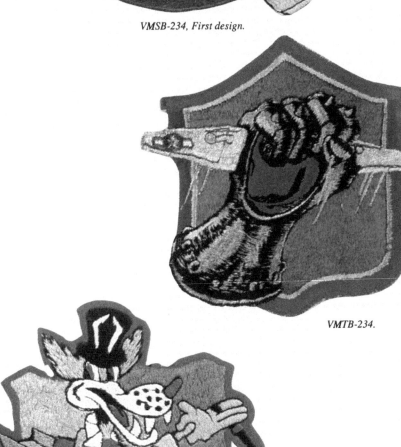

VMTB-234.

VMSB-235.

VMSB-236, First design.

Unit: VMSB-236

Date Commissioned: 1.1.43

Date Deactivated: 8.1.45

Nickname of Unit: Black Panthers

Name of Artist: Capt. Walter Jordin

Date of Insignia: 1943

Authorization: HQMC

Type of Aircraft Employed: SBD-3, SBD-4, SBD-5, SBD-6

Remarks: The squadron designation was deleted from the second issue of insignia which was manufactured in the U.S. A Marine Corps insignia was placed in the upper left quadrant and a scroll with the motto "Vederimus Et Distructimus" placed at the bottom of the shield.

Acknowledgements: M/Gen. Louis Conti USMC (ret.), Col. J.T. McDaniel USMC (ret.), Col. Fred Frazer USMC (ret.), Col. C.B. "Collie" Lageson USMC (ret.)

Manufacturing Details: First issue Australian embroidered on wool.. Second issue American embroidered on twill.

VMSB-236, Second design.

Tom Forsyth on right and unidentified squadron member hold squadron tally board.

June 1945, L/Col. Fred J. Frazer left, Capt. Charbeneau right, flank squadron insignia.

Unit: VMSB-241
Date Commissioned: 3.1.42
Date Deactivated: 8.1.45
Nickname of Unit: Sons Of Satan
Name of Artist: 2nd Lt. Robert M. Egan
Date of Insignia: 1944
Authorization: HQMC
Type of Aircraft Employed: SBD-2, SB2U-3,
    SBD-4, SBD-5, SBD-6
Remarks: none
Acknowledgements: Col. Ben B. Manchester USMC
    (ret.), Donald B. Cooney, Victor Wier, Col. Elmer
    Glidden Jr. USMC (ret.), L/Col. Hoyle Barr
    USMC (ret.).
Manufacturing Details: American embroidered on
    twill. American chain-stitched on wool.

*VMSB-241, Original issue with Latin motto
meaning "Flaming Downward".*

VMSB-241, Privately made insignia with Latin motto misspelled.

MCAS El Centro 1943. VMTB-242 L-R T/Sgt. Fitzpatrick, T/Sgt. Masho, T/Sgt. Lynn, Marine Gunner Mendin (wearing squadron patch).

Unit: VMTB-242
Date Commissioned: 9.15.43
Date Deactivated: 11.23.45
Nickname of Unit: n/a
Name of Artist: Warner Brothers Studios
Date of Insignia: 1943
Authorization: local
Type of Aircraft Employed: J2F-5, TBM-3E
Remarks: none
Acknowledgements: L/Col. John Barnett USMC(ret.),
    Col. Edward Lupton USMC(ret.)
Manufacturing Details: Decal on leather.

VMTB-242.

Unidentified enlisted men wearing VMTB-242 squadron insignia on jackets.

MCAS El Centro 1943. L-R Maj. Dean VMTB-242 squadron C.O., Lt. Mallen squadron adjutant.

VMSB-243.

Unit: VMSB-243
Date Commissioned: 6.1.42
Date Deactivated: 9.21.45
Nickname of Unit: Flying Goldbricks
Name of Artist: Lt. Robert Floeck
Date of Insignia: 1943
Authorization: local
Type of Aircraft Employed: SBC-4, SBD-4, SBD-5, SBD-6
Remarks: Insignia were manufactured and issued to aircrew but not worn as senior officers (not in the squadron) thought it to be in poor taste.
Acknowledgements: Col. John Piper USMC (ret.), Col. J.C. Richardson USMC (ret.), M/Gen. Richard Mulberry Jr. USMC (ret.), Maj. J.L. Fritsche USMC (ret.).
Manufacturing Details: Australian embroidered on wool.

Unit: VMSB-244
Date Commissioned: 6.1.42
Date Deactivated: 6.10.46
Nickname of Unit: Bombing Banshees
Name of Artist: 2nd Lt. Charles G. Fink
Date of Insignia: 1943
Authorization: local
Type of Aircraft Employed: SBC-4, SNJ-3, SBD-3, SBD-3P, SBD-4, SBD-5, SB2C-4
Remarks: none
Acknowledgements: Noble "Buck" Newsom, Keith Dennis
Manufacturing Details: Australian embroidered on wool. Note - the author has seen a version stenciled on enlisted Marine green uniform wool with a serrated edge from being cut with a "pinking sheers". No evidence to support its authenticity.

VMSB-244.

Unit: VMSB-245
Date Commissioned: 9.15.43
Date Deactivated: 11.17.45
Nickname of Unit: Red Mousie Squadron
Name of Artist: Walt Disney Studios
Date of Insignia: 1943
Authorization: HQMC
Type of Aircraft Employed: SBD-5, SBD-3
Remarks: The design created by the Walt Disney Studio depicted s ferocious bulldog standing on a bomb and firing a pair of .30 cal. machine guns-the armament of an SBD dive bomber. In the spring of 1944, while at Ewa, the squadron CO, Maj. Julien "Rockey" Acers, had the Disney Studio rework the original design. A seated mouse was substituted for the standing bulldog. At this time Maj. Acers wife was at Ewa. She was a redhead and he often referred to her as his "little red mouse".It was for this reason that the insignia was changed and "Red Mousie Squadron" added to the design. The "Red Mousie" insignia was not well liked by squadron members. Many disparaging comments concerning the insignia were received at the base EM club and most personnel chose not to wear the insignia as opposed to brig time for fighting.
Acknowledgements: Col. William Abblitt USMC(ret.), Wilton Fleming.
Manufacturing Details: Red Mousie silk-screened on canvas. Disney Bulldog - American chenille.

VMSB-245, First design.

Bill Ablitt - Exec. 245.

VMSB-245, Second design.

Officers VMSB-245 Midway.

L-R: Bill Ablitt & Rocky Acers (C.O. 245).

L-R: Mahafee & Red Norvell - VMSB-245.

VMO-251.

Unit: VMO/VMF-251
Date Commissioned: 12.1.41, changed to VMF 1.3.45
Date Deactivated: 6.1.45
Reactivated: 3.1.51, changed to VMA 4.20.51
Nickname of Unit: VMO-none
    VMF-Lucifer's Messengers
Name of Artist: VMO-Lt. E.H. Railsback
    VMF-n/a
Date of Insignia: VMO-1942
    VMF-1945
Authorization: VMO & VMF-local
Type of Aircraft Employed: F4F-3, JRB-2,
    SNJ-3, F4U-1
Remarks: Excerpt from a letter by Col. Roy T. Spurlock USMCR(ret.) dated 6 November 1985. We (251) departed the United States in June of 1942, and after unloading at Tontouta, New Caledonia, to reassemble and rerig our F4F-3P fighters, the squadron was ordered to the island of Espiritu Santo, in the New Hebrides. At this time there was only one airstrip, partly constructed, which later came to be known as Palikulo Bomber Strip. Our commanding officer, L/Col. John N. Hart, was the senior air officer present, as well as C.O. of the only substantial military unit on the strip. In addition to his own responsibilities and operations, he came by default the only support available to a small contingent of B-17 bombers from the 11th Bombardment Group of L/Col. L.G. "Blondie" Saunders (called "Blondie" because he emphatically was not). This support included refueling and minor maintenance, since the B-17 crews could not fly and do this also; they had not ground support personnel of their own with them. At this stage our squadron did not have the luxury of gas refueler trucks, and all refueling had to be done by hand pump alone. This was bad enough when filling our F4F type planes which carried only 144 gallons of gas internally. With the B-17 it was a different matter, since they required as much as 2700 gallons per plane, and there were

usually three B-17 planes going out every day to reconnoiter the Solomons and surrounding areas. Our enlisted personnel were frequently up all night just gassing these planes, and as time wore on this chore become more and more onerous. This episode was forever memorialized when the squadron insignia for VMO- 251 was designed. The design consisted of an octopus with a pilot's helmet and goggles with two gold wings on a white cloud background. The octopus had only six tentacles (with apologies to our Creator, who gave them eight), and each grasped an item symbolizing one of the functions of that remarkable squadron (there has never been another like it since). The first tentacle grasped a monkey wrench, symbolizing the mechanical aspects of supporting a Marine fighter/photographic squadron which was also fully equipped and served as a radar early warning and control squadron. VMO-251 also maintained an air-sea rescue capability. On to the second tentacle, which clasped a machine gun, which along with the bomb in the fifth tentacle symbolized the ground and air combat functions of the squadron. The third tentacle grasped a camera, which was appropriate since part of the assigned mission was photographic. Each fighter plane was equipped to make vertical aerial photographs, and the squadron had substantial photo-processing capability. The fourth tentacle gripped a pair of binoculars, symbolizing the reconnaissance aspect of the photographic missions. This leaves the sixth and last tentacle. This one grasped a roll of ordinary toilet paper, with which to wipe the Army Air Corps "posterior". It is regrettable that under the trying conditions of war some irritations, aggravations and sometimes outright hostility occurs between services. All of us recognize that such incidents do not really devide us. We were all trying to reach the same objective, which was the defeat of the enemy in front of us." The second insignia was developed to reflect the change in squadron designation from VMO to VMF, the change in mission from photographic - observation to fighter - bomber, and the change in aircraft from F4F to F4U.

Acknowledgements: L/Col. Wendell P. Garton USMC (ret.), Col. Roy T. Spurlock USMCR (ret.), L/ Col. Harry Schwethelm USMC (ret.), Earl McCabe, Capt. R.J. Wallenborn USN (ret.), Col. Ted Wojcik USMC (ret.), Keith Henderson.

Manufacturing Details: Octopus - Australian embroidered on wool. Lucifer - American embroidered on wool.

VMF-251.

Efate 1942, squadron F4F-3 on patrol.

Squadron F4F-3 aircraft parked along side air strip.

68

Earl McCabe home on leave wearing G-1 flight jacket with VMO-251 patch on left breast.

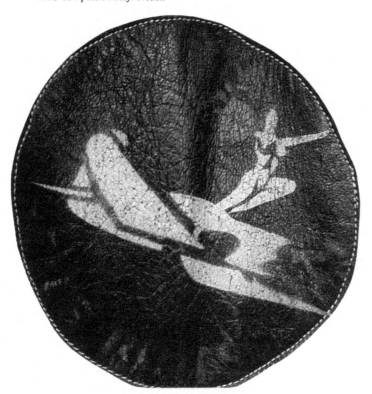

VMF-311, First design.

VMF-311, Second design.

Unit: VMJ/VMR-252
Date Commissioned: 7.15.41, changed to VMR 6.3.44, to VMGR 2.1.62
Date Deactivated: still active
Type of Aircraft Employed: R3D-2, R4D-1, J2F-5, SNJ-3, F4F-3, SBD-3, SNJ-4, R5C-1
Remarks: No record of any insignia.
Acknowledgements: none

Unit: VMJ/VMR-253
Date Commissioned: 3.1.42, changed to VMR 6.3.44
Date Deactivated: 5.31.47
Type of Aircraft Employed: R4D-1, R4D-5, R5C-1
Remarks: used SCAT/MAG 25 insignia, see MAG 25.
Acknowledgements: none

Unit: VMD-2,VMD-254
Date Commissioned: 4.1.42, changed to VMD 9.15.42, to VMP 10.15.45
Date Deactivated: 11.30.49
Type of Aircraft Employed: VMD 2 F2A-2, JSF-5, SNJ-3. VMD 254 F4F-7, PB4Y-1, SNJ-3, SNJ-4, F6F-3P, F7F-3P
Remarks: No record of an insignia.
Acknowledgements: none

Unit: VMF-311
Date Commissioned: 12.1.42, changed to VMA 6.7.57
Date Deactivated: still active.
Nickname of Unit: Hell's Belles
Name of Artist: n/a
Date of Insignia: 1943
Authorization: local
Type of Aircraft Employed: F4U-1, F4U-1C
Remarks: Two versions of the "Hells Belles" insignia were used during WW2. The first depicted a white Corsair against a dark blue background with "Hell's Belles" in an arc below the aircraft. The second version which came into use in 1945 depicted a dark blue Corsair against a light blue background. A Marine Corps emblem was added to the face of the shield. The legend "Fighting 311" was added to the design in an arc above the Corsair.
Acknowledgements: Col. Harry Hooper USMC(ret.), L/Col. Warren Nichols USMC(ret.), Eldon C. Anderson, Paul Goldberg, Bill Thomas, Gordon Strachan.
Manufacturing Details: First issue - silk-screened on leather. Second issue - fully embroidered.

Unit: VMF-312
Date Commissioned: 6.1.43, changed to VMA 6.10.52, to VMF 2.15.54, to VMF(AW) 8.1.63, to VMFA 2.1.66
Date Deactivated: still active.
Nickname of Unit: Day's Knights, changed to Checkerboard Squadron.
Name of Artist: T/Sgt. James R. Wroble
Date of Insignia: 1943
Authorization: HQMC
Type of Aircraft Employed: F4U-1D, FG-1D
Remarks: none
Acknowledgements: Verne Bollick, Raymond Harrold, Former 1st Sgt. Jim Rice, Frank Watson
Manufacturing Details: American embroidered on twill.

VMF-312.

Unit: VMF-313
Date Commissioned: 10.1.43
Date Deactivated: 6.1.45
Nickname of Unit: Lily Packin' Hellbirds
Name of Artist: Lt. William Long
Date of Insignia: 1944
Authorization: HQMC
Type of Aircraft Employed: F4U-1
Remarks: The first insignia were manufactured in Australia during an R&R and distribution was limited to flight personnel only. When it was decided to make the insignia available to all hands, the background was changed from medium blue to brown and all references to the identity of the squadron were dropped for security reasons.
Acknowledgements: Col. Jay McDonald USMC (ret.)
Manufacturing Details: First issue Australian embroidered on wool. Second issue -decal on leather.

VMF-313, First tour.

VMF-313 — 1943, W.O. Russ Kobler, squadron adjutant, outside squadron office.

VMF-313, Second tour.

VMF-314.

Hell's Angels stencilled design.

VMF-321, Disney artwork for 2nd design.

Unit: VMF-314
Date Commissioned: 10.1.43
Date Deactivated: 4.3.47
Reactivated: 2.1.52, changed to VMF(AW) 1.1.57, to
    VMFA 8.1.63, still active.
Nickname of Unit: Bob's Cats
Name of Artist: Walt Disney Studios
Date of Insignia: 1944
Authorization: HQMC
Type of Aircraft Employed: F4U-1, SNJ-4, F4U-1C,
    FG-1D
Remarks: none
Acknowledgements: Frank P. Geralts
Manufacturing Details: American embroidered on
    wool.

Unit: VMF-321
Date Commissioned: 2.1.43
Date Deactivated: 1.28.46
Nickname of Unit: Hell's Angels while commanded
    by Maj. Edmund Overend.
Name of Artist:
    Hell's Angels insignia-Maj. Edmund Overend
    Cat insignia-Walt Disney Studios
Date of Insignia: Hell's Angels insignia-1944
    Cat insignia-1945
Authorization:
    Hell's Angels Insignia-HQMC disapproved.
    Cat insignia-HQMC
Type of Aircraft Employed: F4U-1, F6F-3, F6F-3P,
    F6F-5
Remarks: The squadron C.O., Maj. Edmund Overend,
    was a former AVG pilot and decided to use the
    insignia of his former squadron in China for
    VMF-321. It was used with local authority. When
    submitted for approval to HQMC the insignia was
    turned down as "not in keeping with the dignity
    of the service" and for the use of the color red
    which was prohibited during wartime in 1944. In
    1945 a Walt Disney Studios design was adopted
    while the squadron, with new personnel, was
    training for carrier and close support operations.
    The Disney design also reflected the change in
    aircraft from F4U to F6F.
Acknowledgements: John S. Foster, William H. Bill-
    ings, Vic Smith , Robert Norman, Philip C. Beals.
Manufacturing Details: No record of any patches for
    the Hell's Angels. Insignia were stencilled on air-
    craft and other objects. Disney Cat -American
    embroidered on twill.

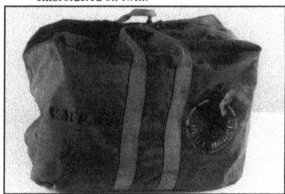

Parachute bag with VMF-321 insignia.

Unit: VMF-322
Date Commissioned: 7.1.43
Date Deactivated: n/a
Nickname of Unit: Fighting Cocks
Name of Artist: Walt Disney Studios
Date of Insignia: 1943
Authorization: HQMC
Type of Aircraft Employed: F4U-1, F4U-1D, FG-1D
Remarks: The design created by the Walt Disney Studios for VMF-322 initially depicted only a buzzard with boxing gloves. When the squadron adopted "Fighting Cocks" as their nickname the design was modified to include it. Still later in the war, when the squadron's mission changed to ground support, the design was again modified. This time it was to signify the squadron's use of the HVAR rocket.
Acknowledgements: Col. Robert Parnell USMC(ret.), Col. John Fischer USMC(ret.), former M/Sgt. Ben Fienga.
Manufacturing Details: First issue American fully embroidered. Second issue painted on aircraft fabric. Third issue American embroidered on wool.

VMF-322, First design.

VMF-322, Second design.

Chimu Field June 1945, John Cessa standing next to VMF-322 squadron sign with original insignia.

VMF-322, Third design.

VMF-323.

Unit: VMF-323

Date Commissioned: 8.1.43, changed to VMA, 6.30.52, to VMF(AW) 7.19.62, to VMFA 7.1.64

Date Deactivated: still active

Nickname of Unit: Death Rattlers

Name of Artist: Art Kemp

Date of Insignia: 1943

Authorization: HQMC

Type of Aircraft Employed: F4U-1D

Remarks: "The incident that prompted the Death Rattler logo was generally as follows: three of our Lieutenants were on the way to New Bern one morning and spotted a large rattler coiled up beside the road in the grass. They stopped, looked, and then one of them returned to the base to get something to kill the snake with. They killed it and our transport NCO skinned him out and stretched the skin on a 6x6 8 ft. support beam in the ready room. I recall the incident well since the snake was about 6 ft. long when stretched out." From a letter by Col. Dean Wilker USMC(ret.)

Acknowledgements: Col. Dean Wilker USMC(ret.)

Manufacturing Details: Decal on leather.

VMF-324.

Unit: VMF-324

Date Commissioned: 10.1.43

Date Deactivated: 10.15.45

Reactivated: 3.17.52, changed to VMA 2.1.61, to VMF 7.1.61, stll active.

Nickname of Unit: n/a

Name of Artist: Lt. Russell N. Monbleau

Date of Insignia: 1943

Authorization: HQMC

Type of Aircraft Employed: F4U-1, FG-1

Remarks: none

Acknowledgements: Russell Monbleau, William Lawhon, Carl Longley .

Manufacturing Details: American fully embroidered.

VMSB-331.

Unit: VMSB-331

Date Commissioned: 1.1.43

Date Deactivated: 11.21.45

Nickname of Unit: Doodlebug Squadron

Name of Artist: Capt. John J. Tooley

Date of Insignia: 1943

Authorization: HQMC

Type of Aircraft Employed: SBD-4, SNJ-4, SBD-5, SBD-6, SB2C-4

Remarks: none

Acknowledgements: Harold Keeble, 1st Sgt. John J. Thompson USMC(ret.), Maj. Frank Takack USMC(ret.), B/Gen James A. Feeley USMC(ret.), Wilton Fleming.

Manufacturing Details: Embroidered on wool.

VMSB-331 Majuro Atoll, October 1944. Pilot John McEniry in the cockpit of an F4U with Doodlebug insignia painted on the fuselage. Corsairs replaced the squadron's SBD's for a few months in late 1944 when the squadron was redesignated as a VMBF (fighter bomber) unit.

VMSB-331 — Majuro Atoll, June 1944. L-R Pilot John McEniry and rear gunner MT/Sgt. Ted Sittel in front of SBD with Doodlebug insignia painted on cowl.

VMSB-331 squadron photo shows insignia which was painted on cowl panels of squadron aircraft.

VMSB-331 — unidentified pilot seated in plane, Pilot Bob Holmes on wing.

Unit: VMSB/VMTB-332
Date Commissioned: 6.1.43, changed to VMTB 3.1.45
Date Deactivated: 11.13.45
Nickname of Unit: n/a
Name of Artist: Francis "Zed" Bowen
Date of Insignia: April 1944
Authorization: n/a
Type of Aircraft Employed: SBD-4, SBD-5, TBF-1, TBM-3
Remarks: "Jack Barnes and I did attempt to come up with an acceptable insignia - while languishing at Midway for two months - but the squadron members didn't seem to show much interest so nothing came of it. However, I did submit a couple of designs." From a letter by Francis A. Bowen dated 23 August 1985.
Acknowledgements: Francis A. Bowen

VMSB/VMTB-332.

Proposed Squadron Insignia.

Unit: VMSB-333
Date Commissioned: 8.1.43
Date Deactivated: 11.21.45
Reactivated: 8.1.52, changed to VMF(AW) 2.1.64, to VMFA 6.20.68, still active.
Nickname of Unit: n/a
Name of Artist:
    Armored Duck insignia-Lt. Edward J. Bender
    Crow dropping a bomb insignia-Walt Disney Studios
Date of Insignia: Armored duck insignia-1943
    Crow dropping a bomb insignia-1943
Authorization: Armored duck insignia-local
    Crow dropping a bomb insignia-HQMC
Type of Aircraft Employed: SBD, F4U-1D in VMBF designation 10.14 .44-12.30.44, SB2C-4 upon redesignation to VMSB 12.30.44.

VMSB-333.

Proposed Disney design for VMSB-333.

Remarks: The insignia designed by Lt. Edward J. Bender depicted a flying duck overloaded with armor in the act of dropping a bomb-signifying the flying characteristics of an SBD and the mission of the squadron. This design was produced as a patch for wear on flight clothing through the Cherry Point PX. About the same time period the squadron adjutant, Paul Blasko, sent in a request to the Walt Disney Studios for a squadron insignia. The Disney Studios responded with a design depicting a crow dropping an egg on a Japanese pagoda. This design replaced the original "Armored Duck" on a squadron sign and is depicted in the unit history published at the end of the war. It was not reproduced as an insignia for wear on flight clothing.

Acknowledgements: Col. Leon Williamson USMC(ret.)

Manufacturing Details: Armored Duck -American embroidered on wool.

DEATH
DEALERS

VMSB-334.

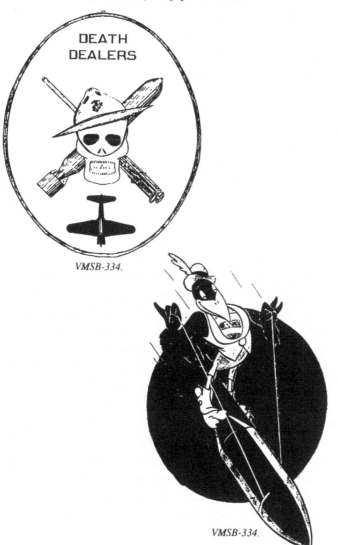

VMSB-334.

Unit: VMSB-334
Date Commissioned: 8.1.43
Date Deactivated: 10.10.44
Reactivated: 5.31.52 as VMA, changed to VMF 1.23.54, to VMF(AW) 1.61, to VMFA 2.1.68
Nickname of Unit: n/a
Name of Artist: Skull insignia-n/a
    Crow on a bomb-Walt Disney Studios
Date of Insignia: Skull insignia-1943
    Crow on a bomb-January 1944
Authorization: Skull-HQMC, disapproved.
    Crow on a bomb-HQMC, approved
Type of Aircraft Employed: SBD-5
Remarks: VMSB-334 submitted two insignia to HQMC for approval. The skull wearing a campaign hat insignia was designed by an unidentified squadron member and disapproved by HQMC. A second design was produced by the Walt Disney Studios just as the squadron was transferred to Newport, Arkansas where it was decommissioned.

Acknowledgements: Col. Bruce Prosser USMC(ret.)

Unit: VMSB-341

Date Commissioned: 2.1.43, changed to VMTB 8.10.45

Date Deactivated: 9.13.45

Nickname of Unit: Torrid Turtles

Name of Artist: Dwayne Ustler

Date of Insignia: 1943

Authorization: HQMC

Type of Aircraft Employed: SBD-4, J2F-1, SNJ-4

Remarks: none

Acknowledgements: Col. J.T. McDaniel USMC(ret.), Maj. John Elliott USMC(ret.), former S/Sgt. Martin Houlroyd.

Manufacturing Details: Australian embroidered on wool.

VMSB-341.

VMSB-341 Cpl. Martin A. Houlroyd, left wearing a squadron insignia, stands next to a family member while on leave.

George Yackee Jr. wearing his well decorated Mae West with a squadron insignia he drew on the right breast.

Cpl. Houlroyd had two confirmed kills as radio gunner with the squadron.

VMSB-342.

Unit: VMSB-342
Date Commissioned: 7.1.43
Date Deactivated: 10.10.44
Nickname of Unit: Bats From Hell
Name of Artist: n/a
Date of Insignia: 1944
Authorization: HQMC
Type of Aircraft Employed: SBD-5, J2F-5
Remarks: The significance of the VMSB-342 insignia is that it shows the journey of a bomb on the way to its target. The fiery red background represents the explosion of the bomb on impact. The bat wings on the bomb represent the speed necessary to get the bomb to it's target. The blue represents the flight of the bomb through the sky.
Acknowledgements: none

VMSB-343

Unit: VMSB-343
Date Commissioned: 8.1.43
Date Deactivated: 6.10.46
Nickname of Unit: Gregory's Gorillas
Name of Artist: n/a
Date of Insignia: 1.5.44
Authorization: HQMC
Type of Aircraft Employed: SBD-5, SB2C-3
Remarks: "Squadron VMSB-343 was commissioned on 1 August, 1943 and ordered to Atlantic Field, North Carolina. At Atlantic Field were two other squadrons in training. Both of these squadrons had names based, evidently, on the characteristics and spirit displayed by it's members and, in addition, incorporated the names of their Commanding Officers. These names also conveyed a certain sense of rhyme. In the course of VMSB-343's residence at Atlantic Field, it too acquired a name. The origen of the name would be difficult to ascertain but it sprang from that common source of most all Marine Corps epithets, the ranks. The squadron was dubbed Gregory's Gorillas.

When an insignia was to be created for the squadron, an insignia in keeping with the name was chosen. The insignia submitted suggests and refers to that name as well as denoting the type of mission assigned to the squadron." Excerpted from the documents submitted with the request for approval of the squadron insignia.
Acknowledgements: L/Col. Walter Gregory USMC(ret.), Col. James H. McGill USMC(ret.), Glenn Kelly, Don Lipsi

Unit: VMSB-344
Date Commissioned: 1.1.44
Date Deactivated: 10.10.44
Nickname of Unit: n/a
Name of Artist: Walt Disney Studios
Date of Insignia: 1044
Authorization: HQMC
Type of Aircraft Employed: SB2C-1A
Remarks: none
Acknowledgements: Tail Hook Association

Unit: VMO/VMF-351
Date Commissioned: 3.1.43, changed to VMF 1.31.45
Date Deactivated: 11.9.45
Nickname of Unit: n/a
Name of Artist: Bulldog in front of flames insignia-
    Walt Disney Studio
    Bulldog riding rocket insignia-Walt Disney
    Studio
Date of Insignia:
    Bulldog in front of flames insignia-1943
    Bulldog riding rocket insignia-1945
Authorization:
    Bulldog in front of flames insignia-HQMC
    Bulldog riding rocket insignia-HQMC
Type of Aircraft Employed: F3A-1, FG-1, F4U-1,
FG-1D, F6F-5P
Remarks: VMO-351 was commissioned as a land
based observation squadron even though all of
it's training was that of a fighter squadron. In
February 1945 the squadron went aboard the USS
Commencement Bay and was redesignated VMF-
351. Another design for VMF-351 was requested
of and produced by the Walt Disney Studios to
reflect the new designation and mission of the
squadron. The rocket in the design indicates the
primary weapon with which the squadron was
now equipped.
Acknowledgements: none.
Manufacturing Details: Bulldog In Front Of Flames
silk screened on leatherette. Bulldog riding rocket
not produced as a patch.

VMSB-344.

VMO/VMF-351.

Proposed design by Disney studios for VMF-351.

VMJ/VMR-352.

Unit: VMJ/VMR-352
Date Commissioned: VMJ 4.1.43, changed to VMR
  6.3.44
Date Deactivated:
Nickname of Unit: n/a
Name of Artist: Sgt. Robert Boyd
Date of Insignia: 1944
Authorization: HQMC
Type of Aircraft Employed: R4D-5, SNB-2C
Remarks: In addition to the insignia designed by Sgt.
  Robert Boyd there are two designs for VMR-
  352 in the Walt Disney Studios archives. The
  duck thumbing his nose dates to September 1943.
  The ghost standing on a cloud dates to January
  1945. There is no record of either design being
  submitted for approval to HQMC.
  The patch which was made from Sgt. Boyd's De-
  sign was paid for by Lt. Tyrone Power, a pilot in
  the squadron, and distributed to all hands.
Acknowledgements: Howard Olson
Manufacturing Details: American embroidered on
  wool.

© WALT DISNEY

VMJ/VMR-352.

© WALT DISNEY

VMJ/VMR-352.

Unit: VMJ/VMR-353
Date Commissioned: VMJ 3.15.43, changed to VMR
  6.3.44
Date Deactivated: 2.15.46
Nickname of Unit: n/a
Name of Artist: n/a
Date of Insignia: n/a
Authorization: n/a
Type of Aircraft Employed: R5C-1, R4D-1, R4D-5,
  R5C-1
Remarks: none
Acknowledgements: none

Unit: VMD-354
Date Commissioned: 7.1.43
Date Deactivated: changed to VMP 11.15.46
Nickname of Unit: n/a
Name of Artist: Walt Disney Studios
Date of Insignia: 1944
Authorization: HQMC
Type of Aircraft Employed: F6F-3, PB4Y-1
Remarks: none
Acknowledgements: Capt. Earl E. Vaughn, USMC(ret.)
Manufacturing Details: American embroidered on wool.

VMD-354.

L-R: Lt. Gerald "Red" Hills, Lt. Earl E. Vaughn.

Unit: VMB-413
Date Commissioned: 3.1.43
Date Deactivated: 11.30.45
Nickname of Unit: Originally known as the Flying Nightmare. This nickname was dropped after it was adopted by VMF(N)-531. Originally unit designation was VMB(N)-413 as they were Night Hecklers. Also known as the Shamrocks.
Name of Artist: Concept by L/Col. Ronald "Fish" Salmon, drawn by Lt. Robert Krider.
Date of Insignia: 1943
Authorization: HQMC
Type of Aircraft Employed: PBJ-1, PBJ-1D
Remarks: none
Acknowledgements: Robert Millington, Perry Wilson
Manufacturing Details: Silk screened on canvas. An American embroidered on wool patch exists but was not employed by any squadron personnel; it was produced for the "Army-Navy Store" trade.

VMB-413.

Munda, New Georgia, July 1944. Sign over air crew mess hall. Signature on sign is L.E. Petty, 73rd NCB.

BOQ MCAS Edenton November 26, 1943. L-R 1st LT. Robert Millington, pilot & gunnery officer wearing VMB-413 squadron insignia on flight jacket and 1st LT. Robert Krider, ground ordinance officer and designer of squadron insignia, trying out newly issued combat gear prior to first combat tour.

Stirling Island, Treasury Group, Solomon Island, April 1, 1944, in front of PBJ-1D. Standing L-R 2nd LT. Harold Kerber, Co-pilot, wearing VMB-413 squadron insignia on summer weight flight jacket, 1st LT. Doug Cowell, and unidentified enlisted crew members.

Unit: VMF-422
Date Commissioned: 1.1.43
Date Deactivated: 4.30.47
Nickname of Unit: Flying Buccaneers
Name of Artist: Walt Disney Studios
Date of Insignia: 1943
Authorization: HQMC
Type of Aircraft Employed: F2A, FM-1, F4U-1,
    SNJ-4, F4U-1D, FG-1D
Remarks: Just prior to shipping out in late 1943, squadron members realized that they didn't have an insignia to take with them into combat. One of the pilots, Lt. Mark Syrkin, called his cousin, Mark Hellinger. Hellinger was a famous Hollywood producer and knew Walt Disney personally. Hellinger placed a call to Disney's home and explained the situation and the lack of time to go thru "channels". Disney told him to have his cousin show up at the studios the next morning. When Lt. Syrkin showed up the next morning there was a package containing 50 hand painted jacket patches which had been painted overnight by the entire Disney Studio staff. A lot of Marines have always said that "Walt was a standup kind of guy". It's very obvious that he was.
Acknowledgements: Col. Elkin Dew USMC(ret.), Col. Carl Schmidt USMC (ret.), Mark Syrkin
Manufacturing Details: First issue hand painted on fabric. Second issue American embroidered on wool.

VMF-422.

Pilot Carl Schmidt wearing G-1 flight jacket with VMF-115 squadron insignia on left breast and VMF-422 insigne on right breast.

MCAS Santa Barbara 1943. Squadron photo showing Walt Disney designed squadron sign and pilots wearing the original insignia manufactured by the Disney Studios, prior to departure for first combat tour.

VMF-422 Pilot Elkin Dew standing next to squadron tally board.

VMB-423, First design.

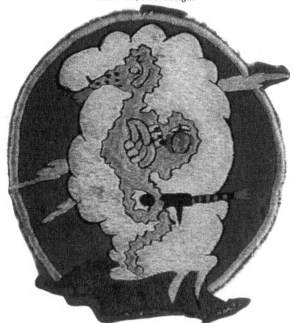

VMB-423, Second design, Australian made.

Unit: VMB-423
Date Commissioned: 9.15.43
Date Deactivated: 11.30.45
Nickname of Unit: Seahorses
Name of Artist: Sheep Riding Bomb insignia-unknown Seahorse insignia-Cpl. Willie T. Phillips
Date of Insignia: Sheep Riding Bomb insignia-1943 Seahorse insignia-1943
Authorization: Sheep Riding Bomb insignia-local Seahorse insignia-HQMC
Type of Aircraft Employed: PBJ-1D, PBJ-1J
Remarks: "The first insignia was a Black Sheep riding a bomb. It was later learned that there already was a Black Sheep Squadron and a contest was held for a new insignia. The winning artist was Corporal Willie T. Phillips and the prize was a case of warm beer. Corporal Phillips was a tail gunner and was killed by ack ack fire on December 23, 1944." From a letter by James F. Lisi, dated October 19, 1987
Acknowledgements: James F. Lisi, Joseph G. Strough, Edward Sofers, Charles Mason, Tom Fitzgerald
Manufacturing Details: Sheep Riding Bomb -decal on leather. Seahorse first issue -decal on leather. Seahorse second issue -Australian embroidered on wool.

VMB-423, Second design, decal on leather.

VMB-433.

Unit: VMB-433
Date Commissioned: 9.15.43
Date Deactivated: 11.30.45
Nickname of Unit: n/a
Name of Artist: Lt. Malcomb McGuckin
Date of Insignia: 1944
Authorization: HQMC
Type of Aircraft Employed: PBJ-1D, PBJ-1J
Remarks: none
Acknowledgements: Maj. Henry Sory USMC (ret.), Vince Montie, Art Boulton
Manufacturing Details: Decal on leather.

VMB-433 — Bombs away! Mission to Rabaul, New Briton, late 1944.

VMB-433 — Emirau Island, 1944. Standing L-R: L. Hoff, Lt. Sory, Lt. Lewis. Kneeling: D. Montie, L. Boulton, L. Albright. Aside from "mission bombs," decoration of aircraft was not permitted.

VMB-433 — Emirau Island, 1944. Standing L-R: Lt. McAllister, Lt. Leonard, Cpl. L. Stebbins. Kneeling: L. Stokes, L. Tatreau, L. Enswiler. Note PBJ-1D in background with belly radome.

VMB-433 — Emirau Island, 1944. Standing L-R: L. Nebis, Capt. Lattner (wearing insignia), Lt. Mennes. Kneeling: D. Warburton, D. James, L. Savino.

TOK BILOG GUVMAN

YU MAS LUKAUTIM GUT DISPELA MASTA. HAITIM LONG OL JAPAN, NA BRINIM LONG KIAP NA SOLDIA BILOG YUMI. WOK BILOG GUVMAN OLSEM, NA IGAT PE.

YU NOKAN SAKIM DISPELA TOK.

(TO BE READ TO NATIVES WHO CANNOT READ)

GOV'MENT E TALK YOU MUST LOOKOUT IM ME. YOU NO CAN TALK IM JAPAN. WHERE STOP KIAP ALL THE SAME SOLDIER BELONG YOU-ME?

SHOWIM ME ROAD. NOW BEHIND YOU CATCHIM PAY.

GOV'MENT E TALK

"Blood Chit" carried by VMB-433 crews.

Unit: VMF-441
Date Commissioned: 10.1.42
Date Deactivated: 7.11.45
Nickname of Unit: Blackjacks
Name of Artist: n/a
Date of Insignia: n/a
Authorization: HQMC
Type of Aircraft Employed: F4F-4, F4U-1, F4U-1C,
    F4U-1D, FG-1D
Remarks: None
Acknowledgements: L/Col. F. C. "Kirk" Kirkpatrick
    USMC (ret.), Col. Robert O. White USMC (ret.),
    Col. Hardy Hay USMC (ret.)

VMF-441.

Okinawa, 1945, VMF-441 Squadron tally board outside the operations shack. L-R. F.C. "Kirk" Kirkpatrick and Tom Hughes.

Unit: VMB-443
Date Commissioned: 9.15.43
Date Deactivated: 11.30.45
Nickname of Unit: n/a
Name of Artist: Donald Graser
Date of Insignia: 1944
Authorization: HQMC
Type of Aircraft Employed: PBJ-1D, PBJ-1J
Remarks: None
Acknowledgements: E. James Beam, Vincent
    Giacobone, Robert Kleckner, Lt/Col. Melvin
    Flaherty USMC (ret.)
Manufacturing Details: First issue -American embroi-
    dered on twill. Second issue -Australian embroi-
    dered on wool.

VMB-443.

VMF-451.

Unit: VMF-451
Date Commissioned: 2.15.44
Date Deactivated: 9.10.45
Nickname of Unit: Blue Devils
Name of Artist: Dorothy Johnstone (maiden name Ramsey)
Date of Insignia: 1944
Authorization: HQMC
Type of Aircraft Employed: F3A-1, FG-1, SB2C-4E
Remarks: none
Acknowledgements: Raymond Swalley, William Peek, Col. Herbert Long USMC (ret.), Dorothy Johnstone
Manufacturing Details: American embroidered on wool.

MCAS Mojave 1944. Honorary VMF-451 squadron member Veronica Lake wearing her flight jacket at the party for the introduction of the official squadron insigne. Veronica Lake is showing the effects of the squadron punch.

Unit: VMF-452
Date Commissioned: 2.15.44
Date Deactivated: 12.31.49
Nickname of Unit: Sky Raiders
Name of Artist: Lt. Norwood Russel Hanson
Date of Insignia: 1944
Authorization: HQMC
Type of Aircraft Employed: FG-1, SB2C-4E
Remarks: "The motif of the insignia is as follows: We have a rugged looking individual waving an extermely large scimitar above his head. It is plain to see that the personage herein described is Ali Baba. This derivation has arisen from the type of plane we use, the Corsair. In Arabic corsair means Thief, thus Ali Baba has been adopted to be our insignia from Arabian Night Fame. The consequence of which it is aptly named, The Sky Raiders." Excerpt taken from the original request for approval of squadron insignia, dated 25 May 1944.

The artist, Lt. Norwood Russel Hanson, went on to become a Rhodes scholar, a professor at Cambridge, and eventually head of the Philosophy Department at Yale University. He was killed while flying his F8F Bearcat in 1966.

The squadron was aboard the Franklin during it's short ill-fated cruise off the coast of Japan when it was hit and severely damaged by a Kamikaze.

Acknowledgements: Col. Wally Wethe USMC (ret.), Mr. Joyce Wethe, Col. Robert Bryson USMC (ret.), L/Col. C.P. 'Pat" Weiland USMC (ret.)
Manufacturing Details: American fully embroidered.

VMF-452.

Posed VMF-452 squadron photo of pilots with squadron sign prior to assignment on board USS Franklin.

Unidentified VMF-452 squadron member standing in front of squadron sign.

VMSB/SMTB-454.

MCAS Mojave 1945. Maj. James H. Clark wearing VMSB/ VMTB-454 squadron insignia on G-1 flight jacket.

© Walt Disney

Proposed VMF-461 insignia.

Unit: VMB/VMTB-453
Date Commissioned: 6.25.44, decommissioned 2.20.45, reconstituted 7.1.45 as **VMTB**
Date Deactivated: 3.20.46
Nickname of Unit: none
Name of Artist: none
Date of Insignia: none
Authorization: none
Type of Aircraft Employed: n/a
Remarks: no insignia produced for either squadron.
Acknowledgements: Nicholas Hardiman, Col. Stanley Titterud USMC (ret.)

Unit: VMSB/VMTB-454
Date Commissioned: 3.1.44, changed to VMTB 10.14.44
Date Deactivated: 1.28.46
Nickname of Unit: Helldivers
Name of Artist: Walt Disney Studios
Date of Insignia: 1944
Authorization: HQMC
Type of Aircraft Employed: SB2C-1A, TBM-3E
Remarks: "The insignia and nickname 'Helldivers' was developed in line with basic precepts of the squadron, and registered with the Bureau of Aeronautics. The blue background represents the limitless sky; the gold triangle and crimson cloak of our 'Helldiver', the colors of the United States Marine Corps; the flashing bomb, our primary mission; and the grinning determination of the 'Helldiver', the resolution to press the attack fearlessly in the face of all odds. Our official nickname 'Helldiver' was derived from the motif of the insignia and the popular name of the aircraft originally assigned the squadron." Excerpt taken from squadron history.
Acknowledgements: Col. James Clark USMC (ret.), Raymond M. Smith
Manufacturing Details: First issue -American embroidered on wool. Second issued -silk screened on leatherette.

Unit: VMF-461
Date Commissioned: 3.15.44
Date Deactivated: 2.28.50
Nickname of Unit: n/a
Name of Artist: Walt Disney Studios
Date of Insignia: September 1944
Authorization: never used
Type of Aircraft Employed: F3A-1, F4U-1, FG-1, F3A-1
Remarks: Aside from the artwork in the archives of the Disney Studios, there is no record of any insignia being used by VMF-461.
Acknowledgements: Col. Elkin Dew USMC(ret.)

Unit: VMF-462
Date Commissioned: 9.15.44
Date Deactivated: 9.10.45
Nickname of Unit: none
Name of Artist: King Features Syndicate
Date of Insignia: 1944
Authorization: HQMC
Type of Aircraft Employed: FG-1, F4U-1, F3A-1
Remarks: The "Hawky Tawky" bird was well known to the American public as one of the characters in the "Snuffy Smith and Barney Google" comic strip. Its ferocity and animosity towards the Japanese symbolized the feelings of squadron personnel. The Corsair on which the "Hawky Tawky" is riding denotes the type of aircraft flown by the squadron.
Acknowledgements: CWO Richard Green USN
Manufacturing Details: American embroidered on wool.

VMF-462.

Unit: VMB-463
Date Commissioned: 7.20.44
Date Deactivated: 2.28.45
Nickname of Unit: n/a
Name of Artist: n/a
Date of Insignia: n/a
Authorization: n/a
Type of Aircraft Employed: PBJ
Remarks: No insignia on record.
Acknowledgements: Col. Andrew Smith USMC(ret.)

Unit: VMTB-463
Date Commissioned: 7.15.45
Date Deactivated: 3.20.46
Nickname of Unit: n/a
Name of Artist: n/a
Date of Insignia: n/a
Authorization: n/a
Type of Aircraft Employed: TBM
Remarks: No insignia on record.
Acknowledgements: L/Col. John Barnett USMC(ret.), Bernard McShane

Unit: VMSB/VMTB-464
Date Commissioned: 11.15.44, changed to VMTB 5.31.45
Date Deactivated: 3.10.46
Nickname of Unit: Spanish Flies
Name of Artist: Donald C. Buhrmann
Date of Insignia: Oct. 1945
Authorization: HQMC
Type of Aircraft Employed: SB2C-1A
Remarks: "The Spanish atmosphere of the insignia is in memory of the squadron's training bases, namely El Toro and Mojave. The torpedo is self-explanitory, while the pistols are to represent the two (2) wing guns on a TBM." Taken from original request for approval documents dated 2 October 1945.
Acknowledgements: Dr. William H. Hunter, Col. Tolbert T. Gentry USMC(ret)

VMTB-464.

VMF-471.

Unit: VMF-471
Date Commissioned: 5.15.44
Date Deactivated: 9.10.45
Nickname of Unit: n/a
Name of Artist: Guy Oliver
Date of Insignia: October 1944
Authorization: HQMC
Type of Aircraft Employed: FG-1, F3A-1
Remarks: none
Acknowledgements: Russell H. Clark
Manufacturing Details: American embroidered on wool.

VMF-472.

Unit: VMF-472
Date Commissioned: 6.1.44, decommissioned 10.10.44, reactivated 3.1.45.
Date Deactivated: 12.24.45
Nickname of Unit: Flying Seahorses
Name of Artist: n/a
Date of Insignia: July 1945
Authorization: HQMC
Type of Aircraft Employed: F6F-3, F6F-5
Remarks: "This design signifies the primary function of this squadron, that of operating as carrier based fighter bombers. It is a caricature of a seahorse with naval aviator wings representing sea going Marine Aviation. The lower dark blue are represents the sea, and the upper light blue area represents the sky." Taken from original request for approval documents dated 25, July 1945.
Acknowledgements: Col. Robert Bryson USMC(ret)
Manufacturing Details: American fully embroidered.

Unit: VMB-473
Date Commissioned: 7.25.44
Date Deactivated: 3.15.45
Remarks: No insignia on record.
Acknowledgements: Col. William Frash USMC(ret)

Unit: VMTB-473
Date Commissioned: 8.1.45
Date Deactivated: 3.20.46
Remarks: No insignia on record.
Acknowledgements: Col. Martin Roush USMC(ret)

Unit: VMSB-474
Date Commissioned: 4.10.44
Date Deactivated: 9.10.45
Type of Aircraft Employed: SB2C-1A, SBD-5, SBD-6, SB2C-4, SB2C-4E, SBD-4E
Remarks: No insignia on record.
Acknowledgements: L/Col. W. J. Carr USMC(ret), L/Col. Robert Scribner USMC(ret).

Unit: VMF-481
Date Commissioned: 4.5.44, decommissioned 10.10.44, reactivated 8.1.45
Date Deactivated: 9.10.45
Type of Aircraft Employed: F3A-1, FG-1, F4U-1, SBD-5
Remarks: No insignia on record.
Acknowledgements: M/Gen. Robert Owens USMC(ret)

Unit: VMF-482
Date Commissioned: 4.7.44
Date Deactivated: 10.10.44
Type of Aircraft Employed: F3A-1, FG-1, F4U-1, SBD-5
Remarks: No insignia on record.
Acknowledgements: none

Unit: VMB-483
Date Commissioned: 8.2.44
Date Deactivated: 3.15.45
Remarks: No insignia on record.
Acknowledgements: None.

Unit: VMSB-484
Date Commissioned: 4.15.44
Date Deactivated: 9.10.45
Type of Aircraft Employed: SB2C-1A, SBD-5, SBD-6, SB2C-4, SB2C-4E, SBD-4E
Remarks: No insignia on record.
Acknowledgements: None

Unit: VMF-511
Date Commissioned: 1.1.44
Date Deactivated: 3.10.46
Nickname of Unit: n/a
Name of Artist: Walt Disney Studios
Date of Insignia: 1944
Authorization: HQMC
Type of Aircraft Employed: F4U-1, F4U-1D, F6F-5, F6F-5N
Remarks: "This design signiifies the firepower of our planes and the warrior-like determination and tenacity of our pilots in flying the F4U airplane. The Indian was selected to represent the American pilot since other allied nations are also using this type plane." Taken from original request for approval documents dated 1 April 1944.
Acknowledgements: T/Sgt. "Si" Hewitt, Plane Captain
Manufacturing Details: American embroidered on wool.

Unit: VMF-512
Date Commissioned: 2.15.44
Date Deactivated: 3.10.46
Nickname of Unit: n/a
Name of Artist: Walt Disney Studios
Date of Insignia: 1944
Authorization: HQMC
Type of Aircraft Employed: F4U-1, FG-1, F4U-1D, FG-1D, F6F-3P
Remarks: none
Acknowledgements: Col. William "Soupy" Campbell USMC(ret)
Manufacturing Details: American embroidered on wool.

VMF-511.

VMF-512.

USS Gilbert Islands 1945. Unidentified pilot with cloth VMF-512 insignia taped on aircraft for home newspaper press release photo.

VMF-524.

Unit: VMF-513
Date Commissioned: 8.15.44, changed to VMF(N) 8.1.47, changed to VMF(AW) 7.26.58, changed to VMFA 8.1.63, changed to VMA 7.1.70.
Date Deactivated: still active
Nickname of Unit: n/a
Name of Artist: Walt Disney Studios
Date of Insignia: 1944
Authorization: HQMC
Type of Aircraft Employed: F4U-1, F3A-1, F4U-1D, F6F-3P
Remarks: none
Acknowledgements: Col. Howard A "Rudy" York USMC(ret), Richard D. Moore, Robert King, L/Col. Thomas O. Bales USMC(ret)
Manufacturing Details: Silk screened on canvas with embroidered edge. PX patch.

L-R Pilots White, Tom Bales (VMF-513 Squadron CO), Greene, Moore.

Aerial view of USS Vella Gulf. Four Avenger torpedo bombers parked on flight deck and the small aircraft parked closest to the stern, an F4U Corsair with folded wings, give a good indication of what it was like to fly off an escort carrier.

MCAAF Oak Grove June 1944. VMF-513. Top row L-R Romsel, Rosecrans, Lomg, Berger, Foley, Wells, Winn, Hall, Wilson, Tebow, Haddock, Smalley, King, Brown, McCaleb. Middle row Feliton, Walker R.E., Seitz, Gray, Derringer, McGinnis, Dobbins, Armstrong, Bales, Tenvold, Stringer, Seiss, Fisher, Clark, Boswell, Greene, Jones, Thacker. Bottom row Wickser, Smiley, Speigle, Moore, Meek, Owens, Dickerman, Kozel, Fenton, White, Walker J.W.

VMF-514.

Unit: VMF-514
Date Commissioned: 2.20.44
Date Deactivated: 12.9.45
Nickname of Unit: Whistling Death
Name of Artist: Walt Disney Studios
Date of Insigne: March 1944
Authorization: HQMC
Type of Aircraft Employed: F4U-1, FG-1, F6F-3, F6F-3P, F6F-5
Remarks: none
Acknowledgements: none
Manufacturing Details: Silk screened on canvas with embroidered edge. PX patch.

Unit: VMF-521
Date Commissioned: 4.1.44
Date Deactivated: 9.10.45
Type of Aircraft Employed: F4U-1, FG-1, F3A-1
Remarks: No insignia on record.
Acknowledgements: none

Unit: VMF-522
Date Commissioned: 4.1.44
Date Deactivated: 9.10.45
Type of Aircraft Employed: F4U-1, FG-1, F4U-1D, FG-1D. F3A-1
Remarks: No insignia on record.
Acknowledgements: none

Unit: VMF-523
Date Commissioned: 5.5.44
Date Deactivated: 10.15.45
Type of Aircraft Employed: F4U-1, FG-1, FG-1D
Remarks: No insignia on record.
Acknowledgements: Col. Stanley Nickola USMC(ret)

VMF-524.

VMF(N)-531.

Unit: VMF-524
Date Commissioned: 5.10.44
Date Deactivated: 10.15.45
Nickname of Unit: n/a
Name of Artist: Emmet Boyle
Date of Insignia: November 1944
Authorization: HQMC
Type of Aircraft Employed: F4U-1, FG-1, FG-1D
Remarks: none
Acknowledgements: L/Col. Donald Bush USMC(ret),
    Willis Robertson
Manufacturing Details: First issue American embroidered on twill. Second issue American embroidered on wool.

Unit: VMF(N)-531
Date Commissioned: 11.16.42, changed to VMF(AW)
    12.1.55, changed to VMFA 8.1.63
Date Deactivated: still active
Nickname of Unit: Gray Ghosts
Name of Artist: Col. John Colby USMC(ret)
Date of Insignia: January 1944
Authorization: HQMC
Type of Aircraft Employed: SNJ-4, SB2A-2/4
    (Brewster Buccanneers reclaimed from the
    Dutch Air Force when Java fell), PV-1 (Ventura),
    SBD-5, F4U-1, F6F-3, F7F-3N, SBD-6, F7F-2N,
    J2F-6, SNB-2
Remarks: None
Acknowledgements: B/Gen. Frank H. Schwable
    USMC(ret), Col. John Colby USMC(ret), Bud
    Ayer, George St. Pierre, Col. Dean E. Baesel
    USMC(ret), Maj. Gen Frank C. Lang USMC(ret).

Nose of "Gertie the Goon" showing early radar probe and ordinance.

Nose art on "Chloe" with victory flags.

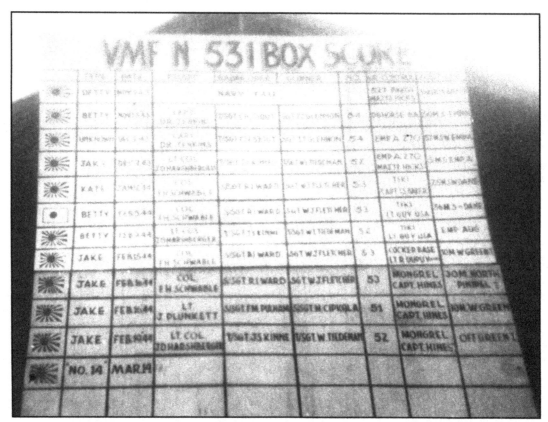

VMF-531 squadron tally board.

Bougainville 1944. "Chloe."

Bougainville 1944. "Gertie the Goon."

Nose art on PV1 "Coral Princess." The first aircraft lost by the VMF(N)-531 squadron.

May 1944, pilot John Thistlethwaite sitting on the wing of "Midnight Cocktail." The unofficial squadron insignia and one victory flag are painted on the aircraft cowl.

Above: VMF(N)-532. Australian embroidered on wool.

Right: Officially submitted and approved artwork for the insignia which was never used.

Unit: VMF(N)532
Date Commissioned: 4.1.43
Date Deactivated: 5.31.47
Nickname of Unit: n/a
Name of Artist: Owl insignia-Edward A. Sovik
Winged Panther insignia-unknown
Date of Insignia: Owl insignia-1943
Winged Panther-1944
Authorization: Owl insignia-HQMC
Winged Panther insignia-local
Type of Aircraft Employed: SB2A-4, SNJ-4, F4U-1, F4U-2, F6F-3, F6F-3N, F7F-2N
Remarks: The Owl insignia, even though officially approved for use, was never used. While flying night cover operations from Roi an ordnance men designed the Flying Panther insignia which was painted on cowls of squadron aircraft. A locally made jacket patch was also produced in very limited numbers for flight personnel.
Acknowledgements: John R Thistlethwaite, Edward A. Sovik, Maj/Gen Frank C. Lang USMC(ret), Col. Ross Mickey USMC(ret), Charles Caniff, Everett H Vaughan.
Manufacturing Details: Winged Panther silk-screened on chamois leather. Australian embroidered on wool.

VMF(N)-532. Australian embroidered on wool.

VMF(N)-532. Silk-screened on chamois leather.

Unit: VMF(N)533
Date Commissioned: 10.1.43, changed to VMF 7.1.53, to VMF(AW) 12.31.56, to VMA 6.1.57.
Date Deactivated: still active
Nickname of Unit: Black Mac's Killers
Name of Artist: B/Gen. Homer Hutchenson USMC(ret)
Date of Insignia: 1944
Authorization: HQMC
Type of Aircraft Employed: F6F-3N, F6F-5N
Remarks: Original design did not have the outer white band on it. The band, squadron nickname, and squadron designation were added when the squadron went to Okinawa.
Acknowledgements: Albert Rose, B/Gen Homer Hutchenson USMC(ret)., Charles L. Schroeder
Manufacturing Details: American embroidered on wool.

VMF(N)-533.

Unit: VMF(N)534
Date Commissioned: 10.1.43
Date Deactivated: 5.31.47
Nickname of Unit: n/a
Name of Artist: Cat Sitting On Cloud insignia-Sgt. Robert Vieth
Cat Kneeling On Cloud insignia-Sgt. Robert Vieth
Date of Insignia: 1944
Authorization: HQMC
Type of Aircraft Employed: F6F-3N
Remarks: The Cat Sitting On A Cloud insignia was officially approved for use on 14 February 1944. The original design was modified and resubmitted. "Squadron members were never wholly satisfied with the present insignia. It was adopted because an insignia was required and it was the best available at the time. The meaning of the insignia has not changed. The self assured cat represents the type of planes we are flying (the Hellcat); the gun, our armament; the evening clothes and moon, that it is night; the cloud, that we are airborne. The whole insignia signifies that we are standing by to catch the enemy just as a cat lies in wait for a rat." exerpted from submittal documents dated 4 November 1944. Approval was given 26 December 1944.
Acknowledgements: Joe Rawlins, John Estabrook, Col. Ross Mickey USMC (ret), M/Sgt. Fritz Gemeinhardt USMC (ret).

Officially submitted and approved insignia design for VMF(N)-534, which was never used.

VMF(N) 534 F6F-5N with VMF(N)-534 insignia painted on cowl.

Closeup of cowl artwork.

VMF(N)-541.

Unit: VMF(N)541
Date Commissioned: 2.15.44
Date Deactivated: 4.30.46
Nickname of Unit: Bateyes
Name of Artist: Pfc. John Keith
Date of Insignia: 1944
Authorization: HQMC
Type of Aircraft Employed: F6F-3N, F6F-5N
Remarks: none
Acknowledgements: Col. Norman Mitchell USMC (ret), Dr. Edwin Rasberry, Warren A Larsen, Robert Marr, John Devine
Manufacturing Details: American embroidered on twill.

Leyte 1945, VMF(N)-541 squadron tally board.

Peleliu October 1944. Artwork on a squadron F6F-5N.

Peleliu October 1944. S/Sgt. Charles Cocco.

Peleliu October 1944. L-R Cpl. William Sykes and Sgt. James Cardis.

Peleliu October 1944. L-R Cpl. Harold St. Martin and Cpl. Ben Stepanian.

Peleliu October 1944. L-R Cpl. Leo Descoteaux and Sgt. Everett Ferrell.

Peleliu October 1944. L-R Sgt. Elmer Bostock and Cpl. George Wong.

Peleliu October 1944. L-R Cpl. Albert Doster and Cpl. Jack Horrell.

Peleliu 1944. L-R S/Sgt. Joseph Smith and Cpl. Larry Pucciarelli in front of "Nancy."

Unit: VMF(N)-542
Date Commissioned: 3.6.44, changed to VMF(AW) 10.18.48, changed to VMFA 11.2.63
Date Deactivated: 6.30.70
Nickname of Unit: none
Name of Artist: Walt Disney Studios
Date of Insignia: 1943
Authorization: HQMC
Type of Aircraft Employed: F6F-3N, F6F-5N
Remarks: none
Acknowledgements: Stubb Hargas
Manufacturing Details: Silk-screened on canvas with embroidered edge. PX patch.

VMF-542.

VMF-543.

Disney design, for VMF-543, which was never used.

Unit: VMF(N)-543
Date Commissioned: 4.15.44
Date Deactivated: 4.11.45
Nickname of Unit: Nighthawks
Name of Artist: Owl With Boxing Gloves insignia
  Walt Disney Studios
  Nighthawk insignia-Milton Caniff
Date of Insignia: 1944
Authorization:
  Owl With Boxing Gloves-never submitted
  Nighthawk insignia-HQMC
Type of Aircraft Employed: F6F-3N, F6F-5N
Remarks: none
Acknowledgements: Col. William Mitchell USMC
  (ret), Col. Robert Warren USMC (ret),
  Clair Chamberlain
Manufacturing Details: First issue -silk-screened on
  canvas with embroidered edge. PX patch.
  Second issue -American embroidered on wool.

Pilot Bob Warren standing center and his plane crew in front of his F6F-5N with the "Nighthawks" insignia painted on the cowl.

Bob Warren, standing at right, wears G-1 flight jacket with the "Nighthawks" insignia on the right breast.

Unit: VMF(N)-544
Date Commissioned: 5.1.44
Date Deactivated: 4.20.46
Nickname of Unit: n/a
Name of Artist: Cleon E. Hammond
Date of Insignia: 1944
Authorization: HQMC
Type of Aircraft Employed: F6F-5N, F6F-3N
Remarks: none
Acknowledgements: Cleon Hammond, Col. Reynolds
    Moody USMC(ret), Donald Grams
Manufacturing Details: First issue -silk-screened on
    canvas with embroidered edge. PX patch.
    Second issue-American embroidered on wool.

VMF(N)544.

Unit: VMB-611
Date Commissioned: 10.1.43
Date Deactivated: 11.30.45
Nickname of Unit: n/a
Name of Artist: Concept by Maj. Prescott "Peck" Fagan
    Drawn by George Connell
Date of Insignia: 1944
Authorization: HQMC
Type of Aircraft Employed: PBJ-1D
Remarks: none
Acknowledgements: Ray Perry, Gilbert DeBlois,
    Robert Jardes

Unit: VMB-612
Date Commissioned: 10.1.43
Date Deactivated: 3.15.46
Nickname of Unit: Cram's Rams
Name of Artist: Black Panther insignia-n/a
    Crossed Bomb & Machine Gun-Sgt. Morton Mandel
Date of Insignia: 1944
Authorization: Black Panther insignia-never accepted
    Crossed Bomb & Machine Gun insignia-HQMC
Type of Aircraft Employed: PBJ-1C, PBJ-1D, PBJ-1J
Remarks: none
Acknowledgements: Capt. George Lenhart USMC (ret),
    Curtis Shelton, Dr. Ivan Roberts, Eugene Kelly, Dr.
    Thomas Honeycutt
Manufacturing Details: Silk screened on canvas with
    embroidered edge. PX patch.

Proposed insignia for VMB-612.

VMB-612 Insignia.

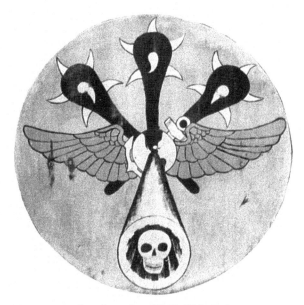

Locally produced VMB-613 insignia.

Unit: VMB-613
Date Commissioned: 10.1.43
Date Deactivated: 10.21.45
Nickname of Unit: n/a
Name of Artist: n/a
Date of Insignia: 1943
Authorization: HQMC
Type of Aircraft Employed: PBJ-1H, PBJ-1J, PBJ-1H
Remarks: In addition to the officially submitted insignia, which was not used, there was a proposed design by the Disney Studios and a locally produced design by squadron personnel. The Disney design was reassigned to VPB-139 on 29 November 1944. The locally produced design, which featured a skull inside a 75mm gun tube, was used on squadron signs.
Acknowledgements: none

Kwajalein 1945, the business end of the PB5-1H. S/Sgt. Staggs servicing 75mm gun tube.

Officially submitted insignia design.

Disney Studio proposed design.

PBJ-1H with starboard radome.

Cherry Point, Squadron inspection with the new PBJ-1H aircraft.

Unit: VMB-614
Date Commissioned: 10.1.43
Date Deactivated: 12.28.45
Nickname of Unit: Ruptured Ducks
Name of Artist: Lt. Walter Dean
Date of Insignia: 1944
Authorization: HQMC
Type of Aircraft Employed: PBJ-1H, PBJ-1J
Remarks: none
Acknowledgements: Maj. Walter Dean USMCR(ret)

VMB-614.

Unit: VMB/VMTB-621
Date Commissioned: 4.10.44, changed to VMTB
  1.3.45
Date Deactivated: 3.10.45
Nickname of Unit: n/a
Name of Artist: VMB Buzzard insignia-n/a
  VMTB Turkey insignia-n/a
Date of Insignia: VMB Buzzard insignia-1944
  VMTB Turkey insignia-1945
Authorization: VMB Buzzard insignia-HQMC
  VMTB Turkey insignia-HQMC
Type of Aircraft Employed: PBJ-1H, PBJ-1J,
  TBM-3E
Remarks: none
Acknowledgements: Ben Moore, Capt. Thomas Kizer
  USMC(ret), Allan Ringbloom, Former S/Sgt. Jan
  Molinari, Edward J. Doyle
Manufacturing Details: American embroidered on
  wool.

VMB/VMTB-621.

Unit: VMB/VMTB-622
Date Commissioned: Commissioned VMB 5.13.44,
  changed to VMTB 1.31.45
Date Deactivated: 1.31.46
Nickname of Unit: n/a
Name of Artist: Walt Disney Studios
Date of Insignia: August 1945
Authorization: local
Type of Aircraft Employed: PBJ-1H, PBJ-1J, TBM-3E
Remarks: VMB 622 had no insignia.
Acknowledgements: Col. David Wolf USMC(ret),
  Richard E. French
Manufacturing Details: American embroidered on
  twill.

VMB/VMTB-622.

Proposed insignia design for VMB-623.

Unit: VMB/VMTB-623
Date Commissioned: commissioned as VMB 5.15.44, changed to VMTB 2.10.45
Date Deactivated: 3.20.46
Nickname of Unit: n/a
Name of Artist: VMB 623-Milton Caniff
VMTB 623-Walt Disney Studios
Date of Insignia: VMB 623-1944
VMTB 623-1945
Authorization: VMB, VMTB-HQMC
Type of Aircraft Employed: PBJ-1H, PBJ-1J, TBM-1C, TBM-3E
Remarks: none
Acknowledgements: none
Manufacturing Details: VMTB American embroidered on wool.

VMTB-623.

Unit: VMB/VMTB-624
Date Commissioned: commissioned as VMB 6.20.44, changed to VMTB 2.10.45
Date Deactivated: 3.10.46
Nickname of Unit: n/a
Name of Artist: VMB-Al Capp
Date of Insignia: 1944
Authorization: local
Type of Aircraft Employed: PBJ, TBF-1C, TBM-1, TBM-1C, TBM-3E
Remarks: none
Acknowledgements: Col. Winton Miller USMC(ret)

Proposed insignia design for VMB-624.

Unit: VML-711
Date Commissioned: n/a
Date Deactivated: n/a
Nickname of Unit: n/a
Name of Artist: n/a
Date of Insignia: n/a
Authorization: n/a
Type of Aircraft Employed: n/a
Remarks: No information on record.
Acknowledgements: none

Unit: VMF-911
Date Commissioned: 6.25.44
Date Deactivated: 3.15.46
Nickname of Unit: Devilcats
Name of Artist: Franklin Jones
Date of Insignia: May 1945
Authorization: HQMC
Type of Aircraft Employed: FG-1, F4U-1, FG-1, F3A-1, F7F-1
Remarks: The squadron pilots and a small cadre of enlisted personnel left Cherry point for Okinawa. Upon arrival Awase field Okinawa squadron personnel were absorbed into VMF 312 along with the F7F's. The Devilcat insignia was used by this group while they flew the F7F Tigercat from September 21, 1945 to February 10, 1946 and prior to their return to the United States.
Acknowledgements: Benjamin Moore, Alfred Wiggershaus
Manufacturing Details: American embroidered on twill.

VMF-911.

Unit: VMF-912
Date Commissioned: 7.10.44
Date Deactivated: 3.15.36
Type of Aircraft Employed: F4U-1, FG-1, F7F-1, F7F-3
Remarks: No insignia per Col. Roy Spurlock USMC(ret), former Commanding Officer.
Acknowledgements: Col. Roy Spurlock USMC(ret)

Unit: VMF-913
Date Commissioned: 7.15.44
Type of Aircraft Employed: F4U-1, FG-1, F3A-1
Remarks: No insignia per "Pappy" Lynch former squadron member.
Acknowledgements: Pappy Lynch

Unidentified squadron member wearing Devilcat insignia.

Unit: VMF-914
Date Commissioned: 8.14.44
Date Deactivated: 1.31.46
Type of Aircraft Employed: F4U-1, FG-1, F3A-1
Remarks: No insignia per Col. C. G. Carr USMC(ret).
Acknowledgements: Col. C.G. Carr USMC(ret)

Unit: VMF-921
Date Commissioned: 8.21.44
Date Deactivated: 10.10.44
Remarks: No insignia per L/Col. Henry Miller USMC(ret).
Acknowledgements: L/Col. Henry Miller USMC(ret)

Unit: VMF-922
Date Commissioned: 8.21.44
Date Deactivated: 10.10.44
Remarks: No record of any insignia.

Unit: VMF-923
Date Commissioned: 9.15.44
Date Deactivated: 10.10.44
Remarks: No record of any insignia.

Unit: VMF-924
Date Commissioned: 4.10.44
Date Deactivated: 10.10.44
Remarks: No record of any insignia.

Okinawa 1945, squadron sign showing unit designation change to VMF-312.

VMSB-931

Unit: VMSB-931
Date Commissioned: 4.15.44
Date Deactivated: 1.31.46
Nickname of Unit: none
Name of Artist: Milton Caniff
Date of Insignia: 1944
Authorization: HQMC
Type of Aircraft Employed: SBD-5, SB2C-4E
Remarks: none
Acknowledgements: Former Squadron Aviation
    Mechanic - Gunner Frank Fortelka
Manufacturing Details: American embroidered on
    wool.

MCAS Eagle Mountain Lake 1944 SBD #18 and ground crews.

Unit: VMSB-932
Date Commissioned: 5.15.44
Date Deactivated: 1.31.46
Nickname of Unit: none
Name of Artist: Milton Caniff
Date of Insignia: 1944
Authorization: HQMC
Type of Aircraft Employed: SBD-5, SB2C-4E
Remarks: none
Acknowledgements: Col. Fred Frazer USMC(ret)
Manufacturing Details: American embroidered on wool.

Unit: VMSB-933
Date Commissioned: 6.20.44
Date Deactivated: 9.10.45
Nickname of Unit: none
Name of Artist: Walt Disney Studios
Date of Insignia: 1944
Authorization: HQMC
Type of Aircraft Employed: SBD-5, SB2C-4E
Remarks: none
Acknowledgements: L/Col. E. R. Hemmingway
USMC(ret), Col. Fred Frazer USMC(ret).

Unit: VMSB-934
Date Commissioned: 7.25.44
Date Deactivated: 10.15.45
Type of Aircraft Employed: SB2C-4E
Remarks: no record of any insignia.
Acknowledgements: none

Unit: VMSB-941
Date Commissioned: 7.15.44
Date Deactivated: 10.10.44
Remarks: There was an insignia created by S/Sgt. Curt
Sarff in 1944. No examples of this design remain.
Acknowledgements: Maj. J.L. Fritsche USMC(ret).

Unit: VMSB-942
Date Commissioned: 8.24.44
Date Deactivated: 10.10.44
Remarks: No insignia as per L/Col. E.R. Hemingway
USMC(ret).
Acknowledgements: L/Col. E.R. Hemingway
USMC(ret).

Unit: VMSB/VMTB-943
Date Commissioned: 7.1.44, changed to VMTB 11.20.44
Date Deactivated: 1.31.46
Nickname of Unit: none
Name of Artist: Cpl. Edwin J. Martin, Jr.
Date of Insignia: August 1945
Authorization: HQMC
Type of Aircraft Employed: TBF-1, TBF-1C, TBM-
1C, TBM-3, TBM-3E, SB2C-4
Remarks: "This emblem employs a grim faced turkey
and an aerial torpedo to represent the torpedo
bomber unit. The turkey is a caricature of the deep
bellied TBM Avengers (also nicknamed turkey
by pilots who flew them because of the tendency
for the wings to move up and down during take
off), in use in this squadron, carrying its deadly
missile to the attack. The background combines
the blue of the sky and a perfect square, both symbols of the perfection that is a vital part of bombing." excerpt taken from the request for approval
documents dated 21 August 1945.
Acknowledgements: B/Gen Henry Hise USMC(ret).

VMSB-932.

VMSB-933.

VMTB-943.

VMR-952.

VMR-953.

Proposed design for VMD-954.

Unit: VMSB-944
Date Commissioned: 4.10.44
Date Deactivated: 10.10.44
Type of Aircraft Employed: SBD-3, SBD-4, SBD-5
Remarks: No insignia on record.

Unit: VMO-951
Date Commissioned: 9.20.44
Date Deactivated: 10.10.44
Remarks: No insignia on record.

Unit: VMR-952
Date Commissioned: 6.15.43
Date Deactivated: 5.31.47
Nickname of Unit: n/a
Name of Artist: n/a
Date of Insignia: n/a
Authorization: HQMC
Type of Aircraft Employed: R5C-1
Remarks: The artwork for the squadron insignia was in Marine Corps archives. There is nothing to support it's use by squadron personnel.
Acknowledgements: Guy Wirick, Col. Stanley Trachter USMC(ret), Keith Hollenbeck, Oscar Hauge.

Unit: VMR-953
Date Commissioned: 2..1.44
Date Deactivated: 5.31.47
Nickname of Unit: Puss In Boots Squadron
Name of Artist: Walt Disney Studios
Date of Insignia: 1944-1945
Authorization: HQMC
Type of Aircraft Employed: R5C-1
Remarks: none
Acknowledgements: none
Manufacturing Details: American embroidered on twill.

Unit: VMD-954
Date Commissioned: 9.25.44
Date Deactivated: 1.31.46
Nickname of Unit: none
Name of Artist: Warren Swanson
Date of Insignia: 1945
Authorization: local
Type of Aircraft Employed: F6F-3P
Remarks: none
Acknowledgements: Warren Swanson.

Unit: TBTU (Torpedo Bombing Training Unit)
Date Commissioned: N/A
Date Deactivated: N/A
Nickname of Unit: TBTU
Name of Artist: Walt Disney Studios
Date of Insignia: 1942
Authorization: HQMC
Remarks: The insignia is carried in the Disney Studio Archives as belonging to Headquarters
Acknowledgements: Walt Disney Studio Archives, Maj. James Durant USMC (Ret)
Manufacturing Details: Decal on leather.

TBTU.

Unit: AWRS-3 (Aviation Women's Repair Squadron-3)
Date Commissioned: N/A
Date Deactivated: N/A
Nickname of Unit: N/A
Name of Artist: Walt Disney Studios
Date of Insignia: N/A
Authorization: HQMC
Remarks: The insignia is carried in the Disney Studio Archives as belonging to MCAS El Centro. The Disney artwork does not show AWRS-3 on the wrench as the patch does.
Acknowledgements: Walt Disney Studio Archives
Manufacturing Details: American embroidered on wool.

AWRS-3.

Unit: I B F's
Date Commissioned: N/A
Date Deactivated: N/A
Nickname of Unit: I've been F…'s
Name of Artist: N/A
Date of Insignia: 1944
Authorization: NONE
Type of Aircraft Employed: various
Remarks: This insignia was designed and worn by a group of fighter pilots who arrived on Espiritu Santo in April 1944 aboard the CVE Savo Island. While they sat and sat awaiting assignment to a permanent squadron, the pilots in the pilot pool were used to check out recently repaired battle damaged aircraft. A lot of the airframes could never be made to fly correctly again and were dangerous in the air, causing more than a few bailouts.
Acknowledgements: Jene Ukena
Manufacturing Details: Australian embroidered on wool.

IBF's

SMS-23.

Unit: SMS-23
Date Commissioned: 7.1.42
Date Decommissioned: 11.1.45
Nickname of Unit: n/a
Name of Artist: Walt Disney Studios
Date of Insigne: n/a
Authorization: HQMC
Remarks: none
Acknowledgements: Disney Studio Archives
Manufacturing Details: Decal on leather.

Unit: SMS-62
Date Commissioned: 4.1.44
Date Deactivated: 9.10.45
Nickname of Unit: none
Name of Artist: n/a
Date of Insigne: n/a
Authorization: HQMC
Remarks: none
Acknowledgements: none
Manufacturing Details: PX patch, U.S. fully
   embroidered.

SMS-62.

Unit: SMS-62
Date Commissioned: 7.1.42
Date Deactivated: 11.1.45
Nickname of Unit: n/a
Name of Artist: Walt Disney Studios
Date of Insigne: n/a
Authorization: HQMC
Remarks: none
Acknowledgements: Disney Studio Archives
Manufacturing Details: Decal on leather.

SMS-62.

*Henderson Field, 1943. Ted Ferguson, USMC, standing next to nose
art which was unusual to find on Marine aircraft.*

MBDAG-44.

1st Mar Air Warring Corps 1943.

MAG-14.

MAG-15 Walt Disney Studios.

MAG-35, 3rd Maw. Walt Disney Studios.

HQSQ-34.

MAG-41, T/Sgt. "Bill" C. Benesch, 1944.

MAG-33.

HQSQ-31.

SMS-15.

HQSQ-41, MBDAG-41. MCAS El Toro. Walt Disney Studios.

HQSQ-61, Walt Disney Studios.

HQSQ 46.

HQSQ-35.

Service Squadron-24 signboard.

SMS-43.

SMS-22, Walt Disney Studios.

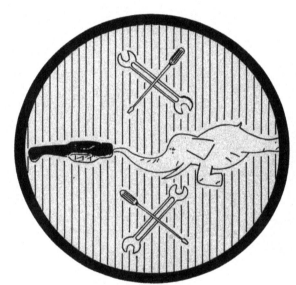

SMS-33.

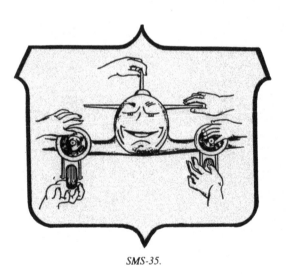

SMS-35.

MAG-24 Service Squadron.

Service Squadron 44.

Unit: MOTG-81
Date Commissioned: n/a
Date Decommissioned: n/a
Nickname of Unit: n/a
Name of Artist: Walt Disney Studios
Date of Insigne: n/a
Authorization: HQMC
Remarks: The design is carried in the Disney Studio
    Archives as belonging to Operational Training
    Squadron #8, MCAS Cherry Point.
Acknowledgements: Disney Studio Archives
Manufacturing Details: Silk-screened on aircraft
    fabric.

Unknown.

MOTG-81.

Piva Airdrome, Empress August Bay, Bougainville, Solomon Islands. M/Tsgt. Sam Lichtman standing next to SBD Operations sign.

SMS-61.

SMS-57.

SMS-53.

MCAS El Toro, embroidered on twill.

Chenille - MCAS El Toro.

MCAS Cherry Point, decal on leather.

El Toro — Baseball team wearing chenille El Toro base insignia.

El Toro — WM baseball team wearing chenille El Toro base insignia.

Glossary

AE–1	Piper "Grasshopper", similar to the NE–1	Galvanic	Code name for the campaign to capture the Marshall Islands and Nauru.
Apprehend	Code name for Dagupan, Luzon, Philippine Islands.	Gateway	Code name for Marianas Islands.
Ash	Code name for Vella Lavella, Solomon Islands.	GB–1	Beach "Traveller", light transport, Army UC–43
AWRS	Designation for Aviation Women's Reserve Squadron	GH–2	Howard, transport
		GK–1	Fairchild 24, Army UC–86
AWS	Designation for air warning squadron.	Glow	Code name for Randova, Solomon Islands.
Backbiter	Code name for Midway Island.		
Beast	Nickname for SB2C "Helldiver"	Goodtime	Code name for Treasury Islands, Solomon Islands.
Battery acid	Nickname for synthetic lemonade, also known as "Panther Piss"	HE	Piper "Grasshopper", ambulance version.
BD	Douglas "Havoc", bomber, Army A–20	Hedron	Designation for air wing headquarters squadron.
Blissful	Code name for Choiseul Island, Solomon Islands.	Horror	Code name for Ulithi Island, Caroline Islands.
Bronchitis	Code name for Kahali Airfield, Bougainville, Solomon Islands.	Hour	Code name for Upolu, Somoan Islands.
Bully	Code name for Marshall Islands.	Housecat	Nickname for "Hellcat"
Buttons	Code name for Espiritu Santo Island.	Idiot	Code name for Suriago Strait, Philippine Islands.
Cactus	Code name for Guadalcanal/Tulagi, Solomon Islands.	Incredible	Code name for Tarawa, Gilbert Islands.
Cartwheel	Code name for the campaign to capture the Solomon Islands, New Guinea, New Britain, and New Ireland.	Inmate	Code name for campaign to neutralize air installations in Truk Atoll, 12–16 June 1944 .
CAVU	Acronym – Ceiling and visibility unlimited.	Ironmonger	Code name for Wotje, Marshall Islands.
Cherryblossom	Code name for Empress Augusta Bay, Bougainville, Solomon Islands.	Jaconet	Code name for Munda, New Georgia Island, Solomon Islands.
		J2F	Grumman "Duck", patrol, amphibian
Cleanslate	Code name for Russell Islands, Solomon Islands.	JM–1	Martin "Marauder", bomber/utility aircraft, Army B–26
Custom	Code name for Roi Island, Kwajalein Atoll, Marshall Islands.	JRB	Beech "Expeditor", twin engine transport, Army C–45
Deadwood	Code name for Jaluit Atoll, Marshall Islands	Kourbash	Code name for Makin, Gilbert Islands.
		Lectern	Code name for Noumea, New Caledonia.
Dilbert	Fouled up individual who could ruin anything he touched.	MABS	Designation for Marine Air Base Squadron.
Earthenware	Code name for Peleliu Island, Palau Group, Caroline Islands.	MAG	Designation for Marine Air Group.
		MAW	Designation for Marine Air Wing.
Epic	Code name for Noumea, New Caledonia.	MADG	Designation for Air Defense Group.
Excelsior	Code name for Philippine Islands.	MBDAG	Designation for Marine Base Defense Air Group.
F2A–3	Brewster "Buffalo", fighter		
F2T	Northrop "Black Widow", radar trainer, Army P–61	MCAF	Designation for Marine Corps Air Facility.
		MCAAF	Designation for Marine Corps Auxiliary Air Facility.
F3A–1	Corsair manufactured by Brewster	MCAS	Designation for Marine Corps Air Station.
F4F	Grumman "Wildcat", fighter		
F6F	Grumman "Hellcat", fighter	Memsahib	Code name for Rabaul, New Britain.
F7F	Grumman "Tigercat", fighter	Mike One	Code name for landing on Lingayan Gulf, Luzon, Philippine Islands.
F4U	Vought "Corsair", fighter		
FG–1	Corsair manufactured by Goodyear.		
FIGMO	Acronym – F___-it, I got my orders.	MOG	Designation for Marine Observation Group.
Flatbush	Code for Vila Airfield, Solomon Islands.		
Forerunner	Code name for Zamboanga, Philippine Islands.	MOTS	Designation for Marine Operational Training Squadron.
FM	Wildcat manufactured by General Motors.	NAS	Designation for Naval Air Station.
		NE–1	Piper "Grasshopper", primary assignment to elimination training bases, Army L–4
FUBAR	Acronym – Fouled up beyond all recognition.		

NH–1	Howard "Nightingale", instrument trainer	SNB–1	Beech "Kansas", twin engine trainer version of JRB, Army AT–11
Nirvana	Code name for Manila, Philippine Islands.	SNC–1	Curtis trainer, varient of Curtiss CW–21, "Falcon"
OS2U	Vought "Kingfisher", observation scout, amphibian	SBW	SB2C "Helldiver" built by Canadian Car & Foundry
OS2N	OS2U manuafctured by Naval Aircraft Factory	SNJ	North American "Texan", advanced trainer, Army AT–6
Outbuilding	Code name for South Pacific Theater.	Squarepeg	Code name for Nissan Island, Green Islands.
Overfed	Code name for Gilbert Islands.	Stevadore	Code name for Guam Island, Marianas Islands.
OY–1	Consolidated Vultee "Sentinel", laison/ light observation, Army L–5		
Panhandle	Code name for Truk, Caroline Islands.	TARFU	Acronym – Things are really fouled up.
PBJ	North American "Mitchell", bomber, Army B–25	TBD–1	Douglas "Devastator", torpedo bomber
		TBF	Grumman "Avenger", torpedo bomber
PB4Y–1	Consolidated "Liberator", patrol bomber, Army B–24	TBM	TBF "Avenger" built by General Motors
		Thorn	Code name for Rabaul, New Britain.
PB4Y–2	"Privateer", patrol bomber, single tail version of B–24.	Thunder	Code name for Zamboanga, Philippine Islands.
PBY–5	Consolidated "Catalina", patrol bomber amphibian, Army OA–10	Turkey	Nickname for Avenger
		U Bird	Nickname for Corsair
Points	System based on time overseas to determine date of return to U.S. or discharge.	Verb	Code name for Midway Island.
		VMB	Designation for Marine Bombing Squadron.
Poppy	Code name for New Caledonia.	VMD	Designation for Marine Photo Squadron.
PV–1	Lockheed "Ventura" patrol bomber/night fighter, Army B–34	VMF	Designation for Marine Fighting Squadron.
Red–Assed	Condition or state of being common to the Marine Corps. Has nothing to do with being spanked.	VMJ	Designation for Marine Utility Squadron.
		VMO	Designation for Marine Observation Squadron.
R3D	Douglas DC–5, transport	VMP	Designation for Marine Photo Squadron.
R4D	Douglas "Skytrain", transport, Army C–47	VMR	Designation for Marine Transport Squadron.
R5C	Curtiss "Commando", transport, Army C–46		
R5D	Douglas "Skymaster", transport, Army C–54	VMS	Designation for Marine Scouting Squadron.
R5O	Lockheed "Loadstar", transport, Army C–56	VMBF	Designation for Marine Bombing Fighting Squadron.
Rockcrusher	Code name for Iwo Jima, Bonin Islands, Japan.	VMSB	Designation for Marine Scout Bombing Squadron.
Roses	Code name for New Hebrides Islands.	VMTB	Designation for Marine Torpedo Bombing Squadron.
RY–1	"Liberator Express", transport version of PB4Y–2, used by CMC (Commandant of the Marine Corps).	Watchtower	Code name for Tulagi–Guadalcanal, Solomon Islands invasion, 31 July – 3 September 1942.
SBC–3/4	Curtis "Helldiver" biplane, scout bomber		
SB2A	Brewster "Buccaneer", scout bomber		
SB2C	Curtiss "Helldiver" monoplane, scout bomber, Army A–25		
SBD	Douglas "Dauntless", scout bomber, Army A–24		
SBF	SB2C "Helldiver" built by Fairchild.		
Scattering	Code name for Okinawa, Ryukyu Islands, Japan.		
Shamrock	Code name for Dagupan, Philippine Islands.		
SMS	Designation for service and maintenance squadron.		
SNAFU	Acronym – Situation normal, all fouled up.		

A Word to Collectors

I realize that by showing the actual insignia as they were produced I have opened the door to those creative individuals who would use the artwork in this book to produce facsimilies of the original insignias and try to sell them to the militaria collector market. Therefore, I'm setting down the conclusions I have reached at the end of approximately nine years of researching this project. All data was obtained through direct personal interviews with former squadron personnel.

Decorated flight gear

Marine aviators simply did not decorate flight clothing the way the flight crews of the Army Air Corps did. The G–1 leather flight jacket was issued to an individual for flight use and had to be surveyed when worn or turned in when flight status changed. Decoration of issued personal flight gear would have been viewed as destruction of government property.

Another reason was that the decoration of flight gear and aircraft was for the most part considered frivolous by senior personnel and discouraged. Also, warm leather flight gear was not needed or worn in the South Pacific. In the humid conditions encountered in a lot of the islands leather turns green with mildew and rots out rapidly. When you see a painted G–1 jacket from a Marine squadron, beware!

Painted leather patches

Aside from the two prewar squadrons which used painted leather insignias, VMF 115 which tried one early in the war and discarded it when the paint flaked off (squadron members were issued cloth versions to replace the leather one on an exchange basis), VMF 311 which had a stenciled leather version, and VMF (N) 532 which had a silk screened on chamois, Marine Corps squadrons did not employ locally painted leather patches because they didn't have access to leather and because leather deteriorated in the tropics. Again, when you see painted leather, beware!

Descriptions of the actual manufacture

Australian made – The patches used by Marine aviation units were all made on wool. Each color in the design was outlined or detailed with a very fine line of black embroidery. The real differences in manufacture become apparent when the reverse side of the insigne is examined. One type of Australian manufacture has a black leatherette backing. The other three types all show thread with an irridescant cotton. When the design is "floated" with the color of the wool as the background color and not fully embroidered, the patch is stabilized with a dark brown coarse weave cotton muslin or a fine weave light tan cotton cloth backing.

Decal on leather – just that , a decal on a very thin leather disc, 4" in diameter.

The PX patch – a silk screened design on canvas with an embroidered edge to stabilize the fabric and keep it from unraveling. The reverse side of the patch shows a black and whitemottled fabric This type of patch was ordered thru the PX system by several squadrons.

U.S. made embroidered on twill – insigne was embroidered on cotton twill material with a loose weave gauze backing like bandage material.

U.S. made embroidered on wool – embroidered designs were "floated" on a wool disc just like the Australian made patches and stabilized with a fine cotton muslin backing.

U.S. fully embroidered – the entire surface of both sides of the patch were totally embroidered, leaving little or no material showing.

Chenille – like the typical high school "sports letter", very heavy looped embroidery on wool.

U.S. silk screened on canvas – insigne silk screened on canvas without an embroidered edge.

Chinese silk embroidery – these patches were manufactured in China and featured fine silk embroidery and pastel colors, on silk fabric.

Australian Made

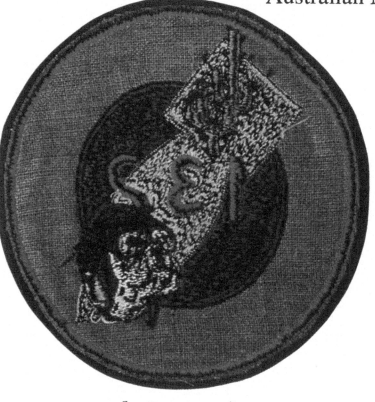

Coarse weave cotton muslin.

Black leatherette backing.

Fine weave cotton muslin.

Fully embroidered.

PX Patch

Typical reverse side of a PX Patch showing canvas with stitching around the edge.

Decal on leather

U.S. made embroidered on wool

U.S. fully embroidered

Chenille

U.S. silk-screened on canvas

Chinese silk embroidery

U.S. made embroidered on twill

Epilogue

I do not consider this research project to be as complete as I would have liked it to be. I ask that anyone having additional information to add, please contact me at Turner Publishing Company. For anyone wanting in depth information about Marine Corps aviation units in WWII, please consult Robert Sherrod's *History of Marine Corps Aviation In World War II* and Turner Publishing Company's *Marine Corps Aviation Association Chronolog 1912-1954.*

TURNER PUBLISHING COMPANY

Publishers of Military History
Nearly 300 titles published with a select few highlighted below

Marine Corps Aviation Association: Close encounters and near misses in WWII and Korea give flavor to this gripping account of these skillfull aviators. Powerful photos, bios, and historical overview give added credence to the heritage of MCAA.

The Corsair Years: "With a vivid memory, Captain Andrew Jones recreates his WWII experience as a Marine pilot of the legendary F4U. His story of one man's war, told with verve and skill, is an eloquent testimony." *James A Michener*

The Battle of Iwo Jima: One of the epic battles between the US and the Japanese. It lasted only 36 days, but the memories will remain forever. Original maps, magnificent photos and personal war stories complete this outstanding tribute.

U.S. Navy Patch Guide: Attack aircraft carriers, battleships, destroyers, frigates, light and heavy cruisers, patrol crafts, 1,300 different ships and submarines from WWII to the Gulf War have their crests displayed in brilliant full color.

The Legacy of the Purple Heart: The Purple Heart - the words alone conjure up images, both sad and glorious, of the toll that true freedom exacts. Preserved in honor and memorial through thousands of photos, biographies and first person accounts.

Other Marine books available: Second Marine, Third Marine, Fourth Marine, Fifth Marine, Sixth Marine, Ninth Marine, American Defenders of Bataan and Corregidor, Chosin Few, and Women Marines Association.